Better Homes and Gardens®

STONE LANDSCAPING

IDEAS AND TECHNIQUES
FOR STONEWORK

Meredith® Books
Des Moines, Iowa

Better Homes and Gardens® Stone Landscaping
Editor: Larry Johnston
Contributing Writers: Don Engebretson, Lynn Steiner
Senior Associate Design Director: John Eric Seid
Contributing Designer: Tim Abramowitz
Assistant Editor: Harijs Priekulis
Copy Chief: Terri Fredrickson
Copy and Production Editor: Victoria Forlini
Editorial Operations Manager: Karen Schirm
Managers, Book Production: Pam Kvitne,
    Marjorie J. Schenkelberg, Rick von Holdt, Mark Weaver
Contributing Copy Editor: Steve Hallam
Contributing Proofreaders: Ellen Bingham,
    Sara Henderson, Stacey Schildroth
Technical Proofreader: Dave Davis
Indexer: Barbara L. Klein
Electronic Production Coordinator: Paula Forest
Editorial and Design Assistant: Renee E. McAtee,
    Karen McFadden

Meredith® Books
Editor in Chief: Linda Raglan Cunningham
Design Director: Matt Strelecki
Executive Editor, Gardening and Home Improvement: Benjamin W. Allen
Executive Editor, Home Improvement: Larry Erickson

Publisher: James D. Blume
Executive Director, Marketing: Jeffrey Myers
Executive Director, New Business Development: Todd M. Davis
Executive Director, Sales: Ken Zagor
Director, Operations: George A. Susral
Director, Production: Douglas M. Johnston
Business Director: Jim Leonard

Vice President and General Manager: Douglas J. Guendel

Meredith Publishing Group
President, Publishing Group: Stephen M. Lacy
Vice President-Publishing Director: Bob Mate

Meredith Corporation
Chairman and Chief Executive Officer: William T. Kerr

In Memoriam: E.T. Meredith III (1933-2003)

Additional Editorial Contributions from Art Rep Services
Director: Chip Nadeau
Designer: lk Design
Illustrator: Rick Hanson
Photographer: InsideOut Studio

Photographers
(Photographers credited may retain
copyright © to the listed photographs.)
L = Left, R = Right, C = Center, B = Bottom, T = Top
Cathy Wilkinson Barash: 158, 159, 160, 161, 162, 163
InsideOut Studio: 58, 59BR, 100, 101, 116–117, 118, 119, 120, 121,
Larry Johnston: 167
Michael S. Thompson: 65T, 67T
Phil Wood: 88, 104-105
Ellen Williams: 9CR

Special Thanks
Hedberg Landscape Supplies
Plymouth, Minnesota

Landscape Renovations
Woodbury, Minnesota

All of us at Meredith Books are dedicated to providing you with the
information and ideas you need to enhance your home and garden. We
welcome your comments and suggestions. Write to us at:
   Meredith Books
   Home Improvement Books Department
   1716 Locust St.
   Des Moines, IA 50309–3023

If you would like to purchase any of our home improvement, gardening,
cooking, crafts, or home decorating and design books, check wherever
quality books are sold. Or visit us at: **bhgbooks.com**

Note to the Readers: Due to differing conditions, tools, and individual
skills, Meredith Corporation assumes no responsibility for any damages,
injuries suffered, or losses incurred as a result of following the information
published in this book. Before beginning any project, review the
instructions carefully, and if any doubts or questions remain, consult local
experts or authorities. Because codes and regulations vary greatly, you
always should check with authorities to ensure that your project complies
with all applicable local codes and regulations. Always read and observe
all of the safety precautions provided by manufacturers of any tools,
equipment, or supplies, and follow all accepted safety procedures.

TABLE OF CONTENTS

CHAPTER HIGHLIGHTS

This chapter shows how you can use
stone in landscaping. Here you'll see
walls, paths, ponds, and other projects
that add richness, style, and function to
a landscape. Design advice and basic
installation information will help you
plan stone features for your landscape.

Stone walls,
steps, paths, and
patios highlight this
idyllic landscape.

DESIGNING WITH STONE

No material used in the creation of beautiful landscapes matches the versatility, impact, and power of stone. Incorporating stone into your plan opens the door to infinite design possibilities. No two stone walls, pathways, or patios can look the same, because no two stones or slabs look the same. Large, jagged stone outcroppings may command more interest than the trees or plants they accent, while a gravel pathway may go unnoticed by garden visitors strolling along it through beautiful blooms.

When stone is cut, chiseled, stacked, or fitted into a landscape design, it demonstrates how skill and artistry can merge with the medium to create personal, artful additions to the landscape.

If you are new to working with stone, you'll soon discover that you can make objects and arrangements with the hard, seemingly inert mass that can advance your landscape to new levels of elegance, charm, and beauty.

EXPLORING THE POSSIBILITIES

The next few pages show the wide variety of uses for stone in landscaping. If you already have a project in mind, find it in the headings that follow, then refer to the page indicated, where you'll find more photographs and design tips.

Pathways *(Page 10)*

Stone pathways can be constructed in many ways, each creating a different look and style as they meander through your landscape. Pathways not only serve the simple function of providing a route through the garden for visitors; in look, size, and style the pathway is an important landscape accent and becomes part of the garden design itself.

Walls *(Page 36)*

Few features in the home landscape match the

charm and timeless appeal of a stone wall. There is something assuring about a wall; it has a look of strength and permanence that is established the moment the wall is completed. Building even the most complex-looking stone walls is not difficult.

Steps and staircases *(Page 46)*

Steps combine simple purpose with strong visual presence to add dramatic focal points to the landscape. Two or three single steps along a gradually rising pathway bring the eye downward, ensuring that the visitor views adjacent plants. A more formal, cut-stone staircase leading to the home's front door offers a stately invitation to enter.

▼ **Stepping-stone paths like the one *below* lend an informal air while a mortared path, *above right*, looks formal and permanent.**

◀ Limestone steps are a point of interest along this path. Stones alongside the slab steps enhance the natural look.

Patios and outdoor living spaces *(Page 52)*

Your yard becomes an extension of your home when you establish outdoor "rooms" that reflect and enhance your family's lifestyle. Stone is ideal for creating spaces for casual dining, entertaining, or simply relaxing with an iced tea at the end of the day.

Container spaces *(Page 58)*

Stone is great for establishing surfaces where you can place containers filled with colorful plants. A pot of blooming annuals set on a small gravel or flagstone floor within the garden bed becomes a dazzling focal point. Stone pillars of different heights, topped with trailing plants in containers, also are dramatic garden highlights.

Garden edging *(Page 60)*

Any kind of stone can be used to edge garden beds, imparting an extra dimension of color and texture. A bed edged with a single course of fieldstone lends a casual, country air to the property, while a raised bed edged with cut wallstone creates a more formal, urban look.

▲ A mortared flagstone patio makes a rustic surface that complements the shingled house.

▼ Fieldstone edging gives this raised garden a wild, informal look.

STONE USES

▲ Gravel, stones, and a variety of plants turn this bed into a rock garden. In addition to being decorative, the gravel serves as mulch.

▲ This stone looks like a natural outcropping because of the plants growing around it. The deck and lamp direct attention to the stone.

Rock gardens *(Page 64)*

Today's rock gardens take many more forms than those of Victorian times. Early rock gardens were usually on sunny slopes and made to resemble windswept, natural outcroppings. Only true alpine plants were used. Now rock gardens can be in any part of the landscape, and can include any plants you want.

Outcroppings and accents *(Page 72)*

Outcroppings of boulders can carry the rugged, permanent presence of stone throughout the landscape. Arrange boulders carefully so they appear to have been in place long before the home was built.

Planter boxes *(Page 78)*

Consider building a long, narrow stone planter box along the edge of a patio. Or two matching boxes can flank the entrance to the driveway or the sidewalk leading to the front door. Usually constructed of cut wallstone, planter boxes can be any size or shape.

◀ A stone planter box filled with bright flowers like this one could enliven an uninspiring corner in any yard.

◀ A fountain is a refreshing addition to any garden. These stacked millstones make a simple fountain that takes little space.

Fountains and water bowls *(Page 82)*

A manufactured stone fountain or a unique fountain of your own design adds an important element to your landscape—the sound of splashing water. Think of stone fountains as audible sculpture; any garden can be improved by their presence.

Ruins *(Page 88)*

Even if you don't have a centuries-old stately manor or extensive grounds, you can have a stone ruin in the landscape. Stone structures built to resemble the remains of a stone wall or structure from generations earlier, ruins become a delightful surprise when visitors discover them in the landscape.

▲ Columns and ancient-looking stonework make this fountain seem ages old. Plants growing over and around it strengthen the impression.

Water features *(Pages 90, 94)*

Pools, ponds, streams, and waterfalls bring the soothing sight and sound of water to the landscape. Water features give gardeners unlimited freedom to create magical, one-of-a-kind landscapes.

▶ Tiered waterfalls in a rock garden make a magical corner in this urban landscape. A pump recirculates the water continuously from a pool at the base of the falls.

PATHWAYS

Pathways not only guide you from place to place, they guide your eyes as well. When designing pathways consider both the practical and aesthetic possibilities within your yard and gardens. Start your design by laying out the main pathways. These paths are the routes leading to and from the house. Where do you travel most in the yard? The main pathways usually lead from the street or sidewalk to the front door and from the garage or driveway apron to the back or side door. These pathways need to be the widest and easiest to walk on; you may be juggling three bags of groceries or some other load as you walk along them.

A 4-foot-wide pathway allows two people to walk side-by-side easily. Guests parking on the street or in the driveway and walking to the house will appreciate this width. Pathways with smooth surfaces and few irregularities are best for guest entryways.

Secondary pathways lead out into the landscape, either branching off from main pathways or existing on their own. These paths can be narrower, with widths as little as 16 inches. A narrow path slows walking to let people enjoy the view.

When choosing pathway styles and materials, consider the materials on your home's exterior. Houses finished in brick, stone, stucco, wood, aluminum, or vinyl siding all have color. The color of the stone used in main pathways can match, complement, or contrast with the house.

◀ Flagstone has long been a favorite material for paths. Plants growing between the stones give the path a rustic look.

The architectural style of the home is another important consideration. Sleek, mortared pathways of cut slate or bluestone will probably look odd leading to an older, cottage-style home. Neither will meandering paths of fieldstone or cobblestones match the mood created by a modern-style home.

The next 24 pages have design and planning information about various kinds of stone paths. You'll find instructions for building paths in chapter 3 (see *page 124*).

▲ Space stones along a stepping-stone path to invite a slow walking pace.

◀ Gravel paths are great for strolling through gardens. They are easy to install and to move as the garden changes.

FLAGSTONE PATHS

Flagstone is a traditional favorite for stone pathways. It comes in various colors and stone types, looks great in all kinds of settings, and is available in a wide price range. Most important, do-it-yourselfers can install flagstone paths that are as long lasting and attractive as those installed by landscape professionals.

Material characteristics

Flagstone is sold under two classifications: *flagstone,* large, irregularly shaped sheets of quarried stone, and *flagstone steppers,* smaller pieces of the same material. Flagstone is generally 18 to 40 inches in diameter. Larger sizes are heavy; more weight than one person should lift. Flagstone is best used for pathways

▼ **Flagstone looks natural in a garden. Plants growing over the edge soften the path's appearance.**

▲ **Flagstones with spaces between them make an informal path.**

that are 3 to 4 feet wide or wider. Flagstone steppers are usually 12 to 20 inches in diameter. They are called steppers because they are of the size typically used in stepping-stone paths. One adult person can comfortably work with steppers. They are best used for narrow pathways, ones 16 to 30 inches wide.

Thickness of flagstone and steppers varies from $\frac{1}{2}$ inch to 4 inches. Stone $\frac{1}{2}$ inch thick should be used only where it will be set in mortar. Flagstone and steppers $1\frac{1}{2}$ to 3 inches thick are standard, and work well for both mortared and dry-laid paths.

Types of flagstone and steppers include limestone, sandstone, slate, quartzite, and granite, so there is a wide range of prices, textures, and colors. Depending on how the stone was quarried, surface texture of flagstone and steppers will vary from nearly countertop-smooth to rougher textures with surface variations around ½ inch.

Design and use

Flagstone is an excellent choice for paths in well-traveled areas. It lends a natural elegance to the landscape and is suitable for both primary and secondary pathways. When flagstone is fitted together tightly and care is taken to create a clean edge, the material matches the mood created by the most stately homes and formal landscapes. Fitted more loosely, flagstone pathways complement virtually all other styles and sizes of homes and yards. Use limestone and sandstone for pathways in shady areas, where the lighter hues of the stone make the pathway more visible (particularly in the evening). In hot, sunny areas, the darker tones of slate and granite create a cooling effect. Direct sunlight will also cause the rich and varied colors of granite and quartzite to sparkle.

▲ Flagstone areas separated by lines of groundcover plantings create a formal look in this garden.

FLAGSTONE PATHS (CONTINUED)

Flagstone is sturdy whether set in mortar or not. Even the heaviest wheelbarrow loads or lawn equipment traffic will not mar or damage a properly installed flagstone path.

Cost

Flagstone prices vary greatly across the country; the closer you live to an area where stone is quarried, the less expensive the stone. Of the

▼ A mortared flagstone path, *below*, is easy to walk on and looks right at home in any landscape. Without mortar the path at *right* looks informal.

types of pathway materials covered in this book, flagstone falls in the upper-middle cost range.

Installation

Scale: 1 (least time and effort) to 5 (most time and effort).

■ Dry-laid flagstone paths: 3.

■ Mortared flagstone paths: 5.

Do-it-yourselfers can install either without much difficulty. Following the step-by-step instructions in this book, you'll find that building a flagstone pathway is an enjoyable and rewarding project, resulting in a safe, solid, permanent addition to your property.

For construction details, see *pages 126–127*.

CURVE A PATH WHEN YOU CAN

Curve a path when possible; curving paths look more natural and are more pleasing to the eye. But a pathway shouldn't swerve just for the sake of a curve; there needs to be a reason to take a turn.

■ The curve could accommodate a tree, shrub, boulder, birdbath, or any object you can route the path around. A curving path through a flower bed looks better than a straight one. Accent the curve by placing tall, distinctive perennials or a shrub on the inside of the curve. A curve or curves can help keep a path on a slope from being too steep (like the zigzag switchbacks in a highway over a mountain pass). A path leading around the corner of a building should curve to provide the shortest route to the side yard.

■ Making a pathway curve so that it disappears from sight lends an air of mystery. What's around the bend? A visitor's curiosity is rewarded when there's an inviting bench, a hidden water feature, a planting of special interest, or an overall change in the vista or style of the landscape to discover.

■ Must all pathways curve? No. Straight pathways lend formality to the landscape, and a formal tone may be the look you want. A wide, straight pathway of flagstone or cut stone leading from the street to the front door of a home (perhaps flanked by columns at each end) makes an impressive statement. If the overall landscape is formal and includes garden beds defined by straight lines, curving paths may look out of place.

FIELDSTONE AND COBBLESTONE

Fieldstone paths have a country look and feel, while cobblestone paths recall the look of long-ago city streets. Pathways made of either material add rustic charm to your landscape.

Material characteristics

Fieldstones are smaller boulders (2–12 inches) formed by the glaciers that once covered great portions of the earth. Glacial tumbling produced small, rounded boulders with a fairly smooth surface. Shapes vary from nearly spherical to egg-shaped or more oblong. Stones in the 2- to 12-inch range that have a somewhat jagged edge and a rough surface are also classified as fieldstone if they formed naturally. Fieldstone is usually granite, though in some parts of the country, small boulders correctly classified as fieldstone can be marble, sandstone, or shale.

▲ Traditional cobblestone paving lends an old-time air to any path—you might expect to hear horse-drawn vehicles and see gas lights.

◄ Fieldstones set randomly into the ground make a rustic path that's ideal for a cottage garden.

Fieldstone color varies greatly. Some typical colors are charcoal gray, blue-gray, brown, red, and white.

Cobblestones were an early form of granite street paver, and are rectangular- or cube-shaped. Large cobblestones may measure 7 inches wide by 12 inches long by 6 inches thick—about the size and shape of a shoebox. The size of cube-shaped cobblestones varies from 2 to 8 inches.

Old cobblestones recycled from city streets are good for landscaping projects, although they are getting harder to find. Recycled cobblestones are most often a dark color. Due to their growing popularity for landscape projects, cobblestones are still manufactured. These new cobblestones come in several shapes, sizes, and colors.

Design and use

Fieldstone paths give a casual, rustic look that brings to mind rural living and small towns. Fieldstone is not good for primary pathways because of the uneven surface it makes. It is a charming choice for secondary paths. Fieldstone pathways look best around older cottage- or country-style homes. They can look out of place leading up to a contemporary home in the suburbs or in urban neighborhoods.

Cobblestones are more adaptable. As a primary pathway leading to an older home, a slightly slumping cobblestone pathway can resemble a charming, nearly forgotten piece of road. Their flat surfaces give better footing. You often find smooth, level sidewalks and pathways made of new cobblestones around expensive, new homes. Depending on the region, they may be called cobblestones or granite pavers.

▼ Widely spaced fieldstones set into the lawn define this path but don't quite count as paving.

FIELDSTONE AND COBBLESTONE (CONTINUED)

▲ **Fieldstone fits right into a cottage garden or rural meadow landscape.**

Fieldstone and cobblestone are best used for secondary pathways. A fieldstone path often takes you from the developed part of the yard to go exploring. Fieldstone works well with informal gardens and wooded landscapes. Consider fieldstone when laying out a winding path to a toolshed, a bird feeder at the edge of the yard, or a compost bin. A fieldstone path is the finishing touch to any cottage garden.

Cobblestones, because of their rustic appearance, can be used in the same way, with the possible exception of paths through wooded areas. Cobblestones were used in the streets of towns and cities, so they look less at home in wild surroundings.

Fieldstone paths are among the most irregular and potentially hazardous. It's easy to stumble on the uneven surface, particularly at night, so consider lighting fieldstone paths. Pushing a lawn mower along a fieldstone path will mean extra work, while anyone driving a riding mower or in a wheelchair will have a bumpy ride. Cobblestone paths are smoother and safer, compared to fieldstone pathways.

Cost

Fieldstone is sold by the ton and is one of the most inexpensive types of stone available.

Old cobblestones are sold by the ton or individually. Just decades ago some cities offered cobblestones free for the taking. Now the stones tend to be expensive, if they are available at all. Contact landscape supply yards in your area for availability. Salvage yards and firms that recycle building materials from old homes, factories, and warehouses might also have old cobblestones, or can lead you to someone who does.

New granite cobblestones are usually at least as expensive as old ones, and may cost more. New cobblestones fashioned out of stone other than granite are available in some parts of the country, and sell for somewhat less than new granite cobblestones.

Installation

Scale: 1 (least time and effort) to 5 (most time and effort).

- Fieldstone pathways: 2.
- Mortared fieldstone pathways: 3.
- Cobblestone pathways: 2.
- Mortared cobblestone pathways: Not recommended.

For construction details, see *page 128*.

VARIETY SPICES A FIELDSTONE PATH

A variety of stone sizes, particularly smaller stones, makes building a fieldstone path easier. Nearly all fieldstones have one side that is flatter than the others. Place that side up in the pathway. Smaller stones, down to 2 or 3 inches in diameter, are good for fitting into the gaps between larger stones.

- Fieldstones don't all have to be the same color. You'll probably find stones that are off-white, dusty blue, pink, gray, brown, rusty red, and everything in between. Don't worry about where you place a stone of a particular color; just grab the next stone based on how close it is.

- Due to their somewhat uniform shape, cobblestones are easy to lay in a tight pattern. Mortaring cobblestones is unnecessary and detracts from their rustic charm.

◀ Set fieldstones into the ground for a natural-looking path. The low center along this path makes it look like a timeworn route.

STEPPING-STONE PATHS

▲ Stepping-stone paths spread all over this yard, creating a pattern and a delightful place for a stroll.

It's impossible to hurry along a stepping-stone path. Simple and comforting, stepping-stones tell all who come to the path that it is time to slow down, relax, and enjoy the journey.

Material characteristics

Stepping-stone paths are most often created using flagstone steppers, small (12 to 20 inches), flat, irregular-shaped pieces of flagstone. Use steppers that are at least 3 to 4 inches thick for extra stability.

Other types of stone can also make wonderful stepping-stone paths. Two large cobblestones, side-by-side, make a fine stepping-stone, as do flatter fieldstones, either a large one by itself, or three smaller stones in a grouping.

Design and use

Stepping-stone paths give the landscape a relaxed, informal character. They do not work well as primary pathways–there isn't enough of a path–but are just right as secondary pathways out and around the yard.

Flagstone steppers measuring about 14 to 16 inches across work best. That's just enough surface area for you to place your foot comfortably. No two steppers will be the same size or shape. Often they will be somewhat rectangular. If this is the case, place steppers horizontally, with their longer dimension extending across the path, not along the line of the path.

For an adult's natural gait, space the stones 3 to 4 inches apart so each footfall will land near the center of the next stone. People on the path will walk slowly, frequently looking down as they place their feet. Placing two or three stones side-by-side, then narrowing to single stones, is a good way to begin and end a stepping-stone path. Create wider areas at points along a lengthy stepping-stone path by doubling or tripling the stone for 3 or 4 feet, making a somewhat circular area. These areas invite visitors to stop and examine a special flower, unusual shrub, soothing water feature, or other focal point.

▲ Stepping-stones alongside the route make a wide spot in this path, suggesting a stop at the arbor seat.

▲ Stepping-stones lead to a mortared dining area made of the same kind of stone.

STEPPING-STONE PATHS (CONTINUED)

Stepping-stone paths are ideal for leading visitors through a flower bed, landscapes extending away from the home, and trails through woods. No other type of path looks more natural and inviting alongside a lake, pond, stream, or water garden. They are also the best choice for pathways in a lawn. A family often develops regular routes across the lawn. Rather than wear a dirt path in the grass, use stepping-stones. Lay the stones so that the stepping surface is at soil level so you can easily mow the grass around and between the stones.

Stepping-stone paths must curve. Because the stones are placed singly, this is easy to do. Even

■ Stones of random sizes make a landing at the end of the path *above*. Stones at *right* are spaced for a leisurely stroll through the garden.

▲ **A graceful curve adds interest to this stepping-stone path. Laid too straight and regularly, stepping-stones can look like a dotted line through the landscape.**

a short path of only five or six stepping-stones can be laid so that the path curves gently left, then right.

Stepping-stone paths can easily handle heavy foot, wheelbarrow, and lawn equipment traffic if the stones are laid carefully in solid ground.

Cost

Flagstone steppers make a relatively inexpensive stepping-stone path. You can literally go a long way with 20 or 30 steppers. Large, flat fieldstones are less expensive; cobblestones are more expensive.

Installation

Scale: 1 (least time and effort) to 5 (most time and effort).

■ Stepping-stone paths: 1.

For construction details, see *page 129*.

BREAK TRADITION, ADD SOME CHARM

The traditional stepping-stone path is made of large, flat stones placed one after the other. But you can add interest to a path by placing some stones randomly.

■ Weaving longer, horizontal stones into the path left to right will create a zigzag pattern that appears natural. Setting smaller stones in clusters, where the foot may land on more than one stone (and occasionally land on more ground than stone) is not against the rules. Vary the spacing slightly between some stones to break up the visual rhythm of the path.

CUT-STONE PATHS

Cut stone—rectangular or square stone with perfectly straight edges—makes paths that look formal and orderly. Cut stone is ideal for main entrances and walkways, and provides a smooth, flat, safe surface for walking.

Material characteristics

Cut stone is quarried stone that has been cut on the top, bottom, and sides by large mechanical stone saws. Standard sizes (in inches) are 12×12, 12×18, 12×24, 18×18, 18×24, 18×36, 24×24, and 24×36. Standard thickness is 1 inch for mortared applications, 1½ inches for dry-laid stone. Dimensions of cut stone are precise to within ¼ inch.

Granite bluestone, a rich, dark, blue-gray stone with varied bluish hues, is the most popular type of cut stone. Depending on the region, limestone, an off-white to yellowish stone with white, yellow, and (sometimes) pink hues, may also be available. Your stone supply yard may offer more cut-stone choices.

Cut stone is sold by the ton and comes stacked on pallets. The pallet usually will have three different sizes of stone, selected from the smaller sizes, middle sizes, or larger sizes described above. But there is no general rule, so it's always best to visit the supply yard to see for yourself. Some suppliers will load pallets with the exact sizes you want.

Design and use

Cut-stone paths have a strong visual presence.
Their geometric shapes give a formal look to
pathways, while their straight edges and
90-degree corners make installation easy. They
work well as primary pathways leading to a
home's entrances or as pathways around the
outside of a house.

Cut-stone pathways look good with most
styles of homes, but they are particularly suited
to newer modern-style homes or stately older
homes. The straight edges and flat surfaces
make cut stone seem more like a sidewalk than
a pathway. Containers, especially terra-cotta
pots, always seem at home along the edges of
wider cut-stone walks.

▲ This front entry path features a
regular, repeating pattern.

▼ Joints are an important part of the overall
look of cut-stone paths. Regular, even joints like
these show careful stone placement.

CUT-STONE PATHS (CONTINUED)

Cut stone is best used in flat, level areas. Laying cut stone where there are even subtle grade changes is costly and labor-intensive. Cut-stone pathways don't curve in the traditional sense. You can, however, make a cut-stone path turn to the left or right by placing a stone to the left or right of the established straight edge, then continuing the path along this new edge.

Knowing the range of sizes of the cut stone you will be using will help you determine the pathway's width and length. Although you can buy or rent a precision stone cutter and cut pieces of stone to nonstandard dimensions, it's better not to do so. Making 4×12-inch or 4×24-inch pieces of stone to make a path 40 inches wide instead of 36 inches would result in a less attractive path; the 4-inch pieces would be out of scale. It would be better to make the path 36 inches wide or widen it to or 48 inches, using standard stone sizes.

Cut stone in this winding garden path creates a striking pattern.

▶ You can install cut stone as a decorative accent. Here it contrasts with the rustic stone steps and garden edging.

A combination of three sizes of cut stone makes a better-looking pathway than using just two or mixing four or five different sizes. Cut stone looks best and installs easiest in pathways that are at least 36 inches wide, and 48 inches or wider is best. That's because there are few ways to mix three sizes of stone in a path narrower than 36 inches.

Cut-stone paths offer the smoothest, safest surface and should be considered if wheelchair access is a factor. Cut-stone paths also handle wheelbarrow and lawn equipment traffic easily.

Cost

Cut stone, regardless of type, is the most expensive stone material. Cut limestone, if it's available in your area, is less expensive than cut slate or bluestone.

Installation

Scale: 1 (least time and effort) to 5 (most time and effort).

Straight edges and 90-degree corners on the stones make installation easy. Larger pieces of cut stone are heavy and require two people to install safely.

■ Dry-laid cut-stone pathways: 2.

■ Mortared cut-stone pathways: 3.

For construction details, see *page 130.*

LET PATH CHANGE WITH LANDSCAPE

Use the formal look and geometric precision of cut-stone pathways to your advantage. Cut stone looks great around the house, but it's less appropriate weaving through woods or informal gardens. Ending a cut-stone pathway—at a clean, straight edge—and immediately beginning a path of different material makes a pronounced statement. It says you've reached the end of the formal grounds; it's now time to explore the rest of the property.

■ Gravel is a good choice for a pathway that begins where cut stone ends. There is such strong visual and physical contrast between these two materials that the visitor immediately sees, feels, and even hears the borderline between landscapes.

◄ Cut stone has been set into the ground like stepping-stones to make this short walk to the birdbath. Broken stones at the corner create a pattern.

GRAVEL PATHS

Gravel paths have been used for centuries in every type of landscape, from the yards of modest farm homes in the American Midwest to the lavish grounds of European manors.

When laid out in a straight line, a long gravel pathway creates a stately, aristocratic look. But simply introducing a few curves gives a gravel path a relaxed, casual charm.

▼ **Smooth river rocks mark the edges of this gravel garden path. The varied sizes and shapes of the stones lend an informal look.**

Material characteristics

There are two types of gravel—crushed gravel and natural gravel. Crushed gravel is stone, most often granite, that has been crushed mechanically. With its odd angles and jagged edges, it packs readily into a stable, even surface, making it the best choice for gravel pathways. It is available in a variety of sizes, from $\frac{1}{8}$ inch to $1\frac{1}{2}$ inches; the most common sizes for pathways are $\frac{3}{8}$ and $\frac{3}{4}$ inch.

Natural gravel is collected from natural deposits, then sorted by size. Natural gravel tends to be quite smooth, even rounded, and often won't pack down properly or remain in place. Consider using it more for its decorative qualities, such as surrounding water features, circling the base of a fountain or birdbath, or in Japanese-style gardens where the gravel is to be seen, not walked upon.

In most regions, limestone and other softer types of stone are mechanically crushed into gravel with pieces that vary from $\frac{1}{16}$ inch to $1\frac{1}{2}$ inches. This gravel, sometimes known as Class II, Class V, or base gravel, also has *fines*, very small or powderlike residue left over from the crushing process. You may also find that wet or dry, fine particles from base-material pathways can track into the house for the first several months following installation. This becomes less of a problem as the powdery fines wash away, or settle farther down into the path.

■ Gravel paths delineate the beds in this formal garden. Although plants grow over the stones along the paths in some places—an informal touch—the straight paths and geometric layout give formality to the edge.

While most often used as the belowground base material for many stone projects, this gravel, when compacted, makes a very firm, low-maintenance pathway. In some regions crushed gravel is available in this form.

Gravel in sizes suitable for pathways is widely available in color blends, mixtures of three or four different colors that complement each other. Depending on your region, you may also find pathway gravel in a single color.

Gravel is classified by size and type of stone, and sold by the ton.

▼ This rustic-looking path could be out in nature. The gravel path with plants growing over the edges makes a stroll through this garden seem like a walk in the woods.

▲ Stone edging keeps the gravel out of the planting areas along this path but doesn't detract from the informal look.

Design and use

Whatever style you are trying to bring to your landscape, gravel pathways will always fit in. Wide, straight, primary gravel pathways leading to main entrances of the home create a sophisticated, European look. Narrow, meandering gravel paths bring a more casual, country feel.

Secondary pathways of gravel leading out into the landscape may be straight and formal, or curved, to lend a more casual air. No stone material installs easier and serves better than gravel across rolling, uneven terrain. Regardless of the size and type of gravel used,

pathways need some form of edging to keep the gravel from spreading away from the path. Though often used, wood boards and benderboard are not good materials for edging. Even when treated, wood edgings crack and rot, and freeze-thaw cycles heave them out of soils.

Instead install the flexible plastic edging designed for use with brick and concrete pavers. This edging can be laid in a straight line or curved. Metal edging is more expensive but adds a more upscale look to the path. Cobblestones, cut stone, and flagstone pieces

▼ Curving along outcroppings, this path helps join the rock garden to the lawn while acting as a buffer between them.

GRAVEL PATH CALLS FOR CARE

Gravel paths require occasional raking and leveling to look their best. If installing a pathway using compacted base material, it's a good idea to crown the pathway slightly—make it higher at the center than at the edges, so rain will drain off, minimizing puddles.

■ Gravel always gets kicked off the path, even when properly edged. For this reason gravel paths don't work well alongside grass lawns, unless you take time to pick errant gravel carefully from the lawn and toss it back onto the path. If you don't pick up the stray rocks, your lawn mower blade will most certainly hurl pieces of gravel toward you and bystanders with great force, at the same time dulling the blade.

▲ **This gravel path with wide spots and points of interest allows visitors to pick their own path through the garden rather than prescribe a route.**

placed on edge make an attractive, more visible accent edging for gravel pathways. Brick or tumbled concrete pavers, set on edge, also make attractive edgings, and are easy to install in curved paths.

Crushed gravel pathways, properly installed, drain well. Pathways made solely of compacted limestone base material tend to puddle after heavy rains. The loose, shifting surface of crushed gravel paths makes them unsuitable for wheelchair traffic and women wearing high heels (and sometimes, men wearing western boots), so gravel is not practical as a primary entry path. Occasional wheelbarrow and lawn equipment traffic poses few problems.

Cost

Gravel is the least expensive type of stone available for pathways.

Installation

Scale: 1 (least time and effort) to 5 (most time and effort).

■ Gravel Pathways: 2.

For construction details, see *page 131.*

MIXED MATERIALS AND MOSAICS

Mixing different kinds of stone and other materials creates a unique pathway that fits perfectly into any landscape. There are few rules for this. Some of the most attractive pathways of this type have been created using odds and ends left over from other stone landscaping projects.

Material characteristics

Where to start? All of the stone materials mentioned in this book can be used in nearly unlimited combinations to create a single path. The goal is simply to create pleasing complements and contrasts between the materials used. Brick, glass block, concrete pavers, round sections from a tree trunk, and even flat pieces of metal—an old cast-iron water-shutoff cover, for instance—can spice up the mix.

Mixed-material paths may be mortared or dry-laid. Mosaic pathways are most often set in mortar, so you can create intricate patterns using the smallest stones. Brightly colored ceramic tile, too thin and light for a dry-laid path, is perfect in mosaic paths.

◀ Cut stone, river rock, gravel, and sand are the main ingredients in this appealing path. Though it looks random and rustic, it follows a definite plan.

▲ Commercial square concrete pavers make a stark-looking path when used alone. Filling around the pavers with gravel blends them into the landscape. Here the gravel fill extends to the edges of the beds, creating wide, casual pathways for strolling among the flowers.

Design and use

Mixed-material and mosaic pathways create wonderful primary paths. Though suitable for all sizes and styles of homes in all locations, they particularly add offbeat, creative flair to houses on smaller lots located in or near a city.

Both types make good secondary pathways. Visitors tend to slow down in order to look at the various shapes and patterns that lie on the path before them.

If you live in an area where a narrow strip of boulevard planting runs between the public sidewalk and the street, consider several short, mixed-material or mosaic pathways running through that narrow strip.

▼ Flagstone steppers set on the ground with small stones between them make a simple, effective path.

MIXED MATERIALS AND MOSAICS (CONTINUED)

▲ Mortared flagstone and exposed aggregate concrete put the off-path seating area *above* on solid footing. A fragmented effect makes an eye-catching corner. Exposed aggregate concrete visually carries a dry stream of river rock across the concrete sidewalk, *below*.

Mixed-material pathways take many forms. Full or broken pieces of cut stone can be combined with fieldstone and gravel to create attractive pathways. Setting flagstone pieces widely apart and filling in the gaps with small, polished river stone causes both the shape of the flagstone and the pattern of the river stone to stand out.

Mosaics take this kind of pathway to an even more decorative level, generally imparting a formal or repetitive pattern into the pathway, with all stones set in mortar. Putting in brightly colored stone and other kinds of materials, such as colored glass and ceramic tile, makes mosaic pathways more interesting.

Mixed-material and mosaic pathways can make guests marvel at the care, attention to

▶ Stepping-stones and gravel create a casual path that matches the informal style of this cottage garden. Plants growing over the edge soften it and draw the path into the garden.

detail, and amount of time that went into construction. Don't be surprised if these pathways cause more comments from visitors than any other yard feature.

Both types of pathways serve wheelchair, wheelbarrow, and lawn equipment traffic reasonably well, although it's best to create mosaic paths in areas where they will handle only foot traffic.

Cost

Cost of a mixed-material or mosaic pathway varies widely, depending on the materials used.

Installation

Scale: 1 (least time and effort) to 5 (most time and effort).

 Mixed-material pathway: 4.

 Mosaic pathway: 5.

For construction details, see *page 131*.

PATH COULD LEAD TO GARDEN ART

Regardless of the kinds of materials used in a mixed pathway, you're likely to create a path with an artistic aspect. Consider introducing sculpture and other types of garden art into the picture, to add to this creative mix.

■ And as long as the pathway is made of mixed materials, why not mix up the landscape it passes? Topiaries, tropical plants, unique shrubs, plants in containers, and eclectic plantings of unusual perennials and annuals will enhance the mood set by the path.

WALLS

Stone walls were probably among the first structures fashioned by man. When people say that a stone wall adds permanence to the landscape, they're talking about more than the impression created by texture and mass; a new stone wall seems to link to all stone walls through the ages.

The basic function of a wall is to serve as a barrier–to contain or to keep things out. Stone walls do this with unmatched durability. The great walls and fortresses of history were built of stone. Sections of the Great Wall of China have survived for over 2,000 years, and Hadrian's Wall in northern England, ordered erected by Roman emperor Hadrian in 122 A.D., remains a popular tourist destination today.

▲ A low retaining wall creates a raised flower bed, a distinctive element in this garden.

To see how a stone wall as a permanent barrier could relate to your property, begin by examining your property lines. Defining and protecting these borders maintains the functional tradition of stone walls.

▼ Low and solid, this wall marks the property line but doesn't close off what's beyond.

Visualize a 3- or 4-foot-high stone wall along the front edge of your yard, where it borders the street. If that seems too heavy and forbidding, consider how the wall would look if it was set back 4 feet from the street. This would provide room to plant a colorful strip of garden in front of the wall, making it more gracious.

Create an entrance in the wall, near the center, or wherever it is natural for visitors to enter the yard from the street. The entrance might include a wooden arch or arbor, or a steel or wooden gate. Sometimes nothing more than a little extra height–perhaps stone pillars–on each side of the opening is enough. Add a stone path leading from this entrance through the yard to the front door.

Borders between your property and neighboring ones are choice locations for stone walls. Fences are usually built along these lot lines, but stone walls are more attractive and they require little or no maintenance.

Stone walls can also be used to define "rooms" or areas within the yard or landscape. These interior walls need not be high–a 2-foot stone wall curving along the edge of a patio creates a more alluring space for dining or relaxing than a patio that simply ends at the edge of the lawn.

The next eight pages explore these and other uses for stone walls. Though not a quick and easy project, building a stone wall is not complicated. Countless stone walls have been built before, so yours will add to the great worldwide tradition of stone walls and, like them, may well stand for centuries.

▲ Terraced plantings with stone retaining walls flank the steps to the entry of this front yard. The lower walls mark the property edge.

RETAINING WALLS

Stone retaining walls combine practical function with artistic form. While important, the main goal of the wall—to keep the earth behind it from spilling or sliding forward—should not be the only design consideration. A stone retaining wall will always be a major focal point in any landscape. Its height, length, contour, and type of stone used offer numerous design options.

Material characteristics

Many types of stone can be used in a retaining wall, provided the individual stones are large enough and heavy enough to remain in place.

Fieldstone

Fieldstone is smooth, round to oblong-shaped granite ranging from 6 to 24 inches in diameter, although fieldstone boulders can be much larger. It is sold by the ton.

Wallstone

Wallstone comes in a variety of sizes, but usually is a quarried limestone that has been cut

▲ A retaining wall leans slightly into the ground it holds up. This low, dry-laid wall is just right for a raised flower bed

▶ Retaining walls often support natural slopes or grade changes. This one contains a raised planting area created to relieve a flat area.

▲ This sturdy mortared wall is a distinctive feature of the landscape. It holds a natural slope that has been terraced.

into rough blocks 8 to 10 inches wide by 2 to 6 inches thick. Random lengths range from 8 inches to more than 2 feet. Wallstone is sold by the ton on pallets. It's best to arrange delivery with the landscape supply yard. If the project area is not near the driveway or street, ask the dealer to bring equipment with the stone so the pallets can be dropped where the stone will be used.

Flagstone

Flagstone comes in large sheets of stone varying in thickness from ¾ inch to 4 inches. Quartz, granite, and limestone are common types of flagstone. Sheets can be as large as 40 inches across. Flagstone steppers are smaller pieces of flagstone, generally from 10 to 20 inches across. Flagstone is sold by the ton and is transported on pallets.

RETAINING WALLS (CONTINUED)

Design and use

Fieldstone

Fieldstone makes an attractive wall adaptable to all types of homes and landscape styles in urban, suburban, or rural settings, as shown by the photos on these pages. A low fieldstone retaining wall like the one in the photo at *right* is the simplest for do-it-yourself construction. The weight of the stones is a limiting factor. Two adults can lift and place fieldstones that weigh up to 200 pounds. (There's rarely room for a third person to be much help in lifting and placing rounded fieldstones.) If your wall will be 4 feet tall or taller, hire a professional landscape contractor specializing in retaining walls. That's because fieldstones large enough to anchor the first, ground-level course of a retaining wall that tall can weigh more than 400 pounds. The second course requires 300- to 400-pound boulders. Setting stones that heavy calls for an experienced contractor with the proper equipment. Stones weighing 200 pounds—the maximum for manual placement—are out of scale as the second course on a wall anchored by 400-pound boulders.

■ The formal look of the mortared wall *below* and the casual aspect of the stacked stones *above right* help these walls fit into the surroundings.

Wallstone

Wallstone makes a more refined looking wall. This type fits city properties particularly well, although if you like the look, you can use it with any home or landscape style. Wallstone is limestone cut into random-length blocks 8 to 10 inches wide by 2 to 6 inches thick. The thickness usually isn't uniform, so it's a good idea to unstack the wallstone from its pallets and sort the pieces by thickness before beginning construction. You can build each course using stone of the same thickness to retain uniform horizontal layers. Or you can mix stones of varying thickness to create what many consider a more attractive wall, but it will take more time and effort to build a top course that is even.

One advantage of building with wallstone is that one person can lift and place even the largest stones. However, unlike fieldstone, wallstone sometimes needs to be broken to proper length (and angle for curving walls and capstones). Breaking wallstones by scoring and splitting with a chisel and hand anvil is laborious. You can break them more easily if you rent a hydraulic splitter (see *page 103*).

Flagstone

Flagstone creates a beautiful, rustic-looking retaining wall, and has been used for walls since the turn of the last century. Flagstone steppers are easier to use than larger flagstones, which must be broken to maintain a uniform wall thickness. Flagstone steppers range from ¾ inch to 4 inches in thickness. It is nearly impossible to maintain horizontal courses in a flagstone retaining wall. It's much easier to fit the flagstones without regard to thickness, then choose pieces to create a level top course.

Cost

Fieldstone is the least expensive stone for walls. Cost of cut wallstone and flagstone varies widely, depending on the type of stone quarried. In general a retaining wall built of wallstone will cost less than one made of flagstone.

◀ Rustic latticework along the top of a low wall adds an element of style to this garden.

Installation

Scale: 1 (least time and effort) to 5 (most time and effort).

- Fieldstone retaining wall: 1.
- Wallstone retaining wall: 3.
- Flagstone retaining wall: 3.

For construction details, see *pages 132–133*.

CONSULT A PRO FOR A TALL WALL

Never underestimate the engineering required for a retaining wall. The topography and type of soil behind the wall are important factors. Building a low retaining wall to create a raised planting bed at the foot of a gentle slope is much different than building a 5-foot wall to hold back the cut left after excavating a driveway through a steep hill. Hire a professional engineer or designer to design and build a wall that will stay in place.

FREESTANDING WALLS

Freestanding walls divide spaces and become important, visible landscape features. Too often homeowners look at their yards and see only the property lines as suitable locations for freestanding walls. But a wall can be constructed anywhere and for any reason. Walls within your landscape can create garden rooms, add privacy or definition to a patio, separate a yard or garden from wooded areas, or hide unsightly equipment or structures, such as an air conditioner or compost bin.

Material characteristics

Many types of stone are suitable for freestanding stone walls. Some types of stone work better mortared, some are best if the wall is dry-stacked (unmortared). Some work equally well mortared or dry-stacked.

Fieldstone

Fieldstone is a smooth, round to oblong-shaped granite ranging from 6 to 24 inches in diameter, although fieldstone boulders are often much larger. Color varies across a wide range. Fieldstone is sold by the ton. Small quantities can be loaded into a pickup or trailer, but it's better to have the stone supply yard deliver large quantities.

Wallstone

Wallstone is usually quarried limestone that has been cut into rough blocks measuring 8 to 10 inches wide by 2 to 6 inches thick. The blocks come in random lengths, usually ranging from 8 inches to more than 2 feet. Wallstone colors generally fall in the white to yellow range, though browns and reddish browns may be available, depending on your region. Wallstone is sold by the ton and is transported on pallets.

Flagstone

Flagstone comes in large sheets of stone varying

▶ A classic stone wall looks solid and permanent. Over time, stone weathers and plants grow up and over the wall to soften the effect.

◄ A low fieldstone wall topped with a wooden fence encloses this yard. The stone foundation makes the fence look substantial.

from ¾ inch to 4 inches thick. Quartz, granite, and limestone are common types of flagstone. Sheets can be as large as 40 inches across. Flagstone steppers are smaller pieces of flagstone, generally 10 to 20 inches across. The color of flagstone varies widely depending on stone type. Flagstone is sold by the ton and is packed on pallets.

Traprock and riprap

Traprock is rough-quarried granite. Rocks usually weigh from 100 to more than 500 pounds. The rocks have sharp angles and jagged shapes. Riprap is the same thing in smaller pieces. Riprap rocks weigh from 20 to 80 pounds. Color ranges from gray to blue-gray to pinkish gray. It is sold by the ton.

Design and Use

When building a freestanding wall, you are actually building two walls—the outer faces of the wall—then filling in the center with rubble and bonding stones.

Fieldstone

A fieldstone wall is adaptable to all types of landscapes and homes. Consider constructing a low, dry-stack fieldstone wall as a divider anywhere you want to change the look or use of the property. Fieldstone walls can be unstable, so freestanding fieldstone walls are often mortared. Dry-stacked fieldstone walls should be no taller than 4 feet.

▼ This gracefully curved flagstone wall sets off the patio and incorporates a small fountain.

FREESTANDING WALLS (CONTINUED)

▶ A rustic-looking stone wall with rambling roses gives a timeless look of enchantment to this yard.

the same thickness to make uniform horizontal layers, or mix stones of varying thickness. Random thicknesses make an attractive wall, but more time and effort is required to lay a level and even top course.

Wallstone is relatively easy to handle; one person can lift and place even the largest stones. However, unlike fieldstone, wallstones must be broken to the length you need by scoring the stone and breaking it off with a chisel and hand anvil. This laborious process can be simplified by renting a hydraulic splitter (see *page 103*).

Wallstone

For a more orderly look, build with wallstone. As with fieldstone, wallstone works well in all types of landscapes and with most home styles. Wallstone is suitable for mortared or dry-stack construction. The stone's cut faces look more uniform, although thickness is rarely exactly uniform. When you buy wallstone, sort it by thickness before you begin the project. Then you can either build each course with stones of

Flagstone

Flagstone makes beautiful, natural-looking walls. Flagstone steppers are easier to work with than larger flagstones, which must be broken into wall-size slabs. Differences in thickness make it nearly impossible to build a flagstone wall with exactly horizontal courses. It's much easier to fit the flagstones without regard to thickness, then choose pieces to create a level top course.

▶ Stone courses in flagstone walls are not uniform or level, but the top course can be made level.

DECORATING OPPORTUNITIES

Your new wall may be so beautiful you hate to hide it, but the new vertical surface paves the way for many exterior decorating options, including climbing plants. Contrasts among plant foliage, the texture of the stone, and the colors of flowers and the rock offer almost endless possibilities. Plants that do well climbing on or growing from walls are described in chapter 4.

▲ This stone wall surrounds a cottage garden and is topped with a trellis that gives plants a place to climb.

Flagstone is suitable for mortared or dry-stack construction.

Traprock or Riprap

Jagged traprock creates a rugged, multifaceted wall that looks like it belongs in the wilderness. The walls are effective when combined with matching outcroppings (see *page 72*) in the landscape. Traprock walls are easy to build because gaps and spaces can be filled with smaller riprap rocks. Traprock walls may be mortared, but they look best when dry-stacked. Traprock locks together in a dry-stacked wall, making the wall more stable than one made of fieldstone.

Cost

Fieldstone and traprock are the most economical stone for walls. The cost of cut wallstone and flagstone varies, depending on the type of stone quarried in your area. Wallstone usually costs less than flagstone.

Installation

Scale: 1 (least time and effort) to 5 (most time and effort).

- Fieldstone freestanding wall: 2.
- Wallstone freestanding wall: 3.
- Flagstone freestanding wall: 3.
- Traprock freestanding wall: 1.

For construction details, see *pages 134–135*.

STEPS AND STAIRCASES

Stone steps and staircases are great design elements for any landscape. They also make it easier to walk on sloping paths and walkways. Wherever you find yourself leaning forward noticeably as you walk up a pathway or when most of your weight is on your toes and the balls of your feet, you are probably on a slope of 10 degrees or more, which needs steps. This can translate into a great opportunity for enhancing your landscape with stone steps or staircases. They not only make passage easier and safer, they also create a sense of transition and provide a strong focal point.

Steps are flat stone surfaces set randomly (or, at least, less than uniformly). You can have any number of steps. Staircases are constructions of three or more steps with the same thickness, rise, and tread (see *page 136*).

Breaking up a gentle rise or fall in a pathway with one or more randomly spaced stone steps makes the path look more appealing. A set of formal stone steps dug into a steep rise shows visitors that the landscape is well planned and improved. Stone steps and staircases add impact to any landscape, and most people enjoy climbing them.

◀ **Steps that look like they lead to high adventure add excitement to this garden. Stones and plants combine for this exotic look.**

▲ A staircase with formal sides makes an elegant approach to the patio from the garden.

As your feet follow steps, so do your eyes. Steps can direct visitors' attention to parts of the garden you want to be noticed. Multiple steps and staircases create strong horizontal lines that add geometric order to the landscape. As with pathways, you can grow a variety of plants in the spaces between and around steps and staircases. Landings on a flight of steps make great places for planting containers, benches, art, and other accessories to interest the garden visitor and delight the eye.

Outdoor lighting highlights steps and staircases, and enhances stairway safety at night. The reflections and shadows from the edges and angles of the stone give steps and staircases a completely different look from their appearance during the day.

▼ Big slabs of stone make a rustic staircase from the sundeck to the pool.

STEPS

▲ Flagstone steps beyond a rustic gate and arbor make an inviting and mysterious passage for garden visitors.

▲ Plants grow over these steps that also provide a spot for a potted plant.

Material characteristics

Thick slabs of stone (4 to 8 inches) broken into widths suitable for steps are available at stone supply yards. Limestone, bluestone, sandstone, and granite steps are all commonly available in random lengths. Some stone yards will make steps to custom sizes.

For less formal steps, such as where a gently rising pathway needs only a step or two, flagstone steppers or relatively flat pieces of traprock make good landscape steps.

Stone steps are often priced by the square foot of surface area, although in some regions they are priced by weight. They are transported on pallets, one to four steps per pallet, depending on their size.

Design and use

Incorporate steps into any pathway with a slope greater than 10 degrees. For a relatively short pathway, you may need only a few individual steps. Space the steps uniformly for a formal look. To maintain an informal look and feel in the landscape, space the steps more randomly. A step connected to a landing is a gentle way to break up a slope. A landing can be a large flat piece of stone or a combination of stones.

The rise from one step to another must be uniform wherever you place two or more steps together. Step height must be consistent because people expect it to be the same for each step. That's why varying the height between steps by even a fraction of an inch can cause a stumble. Install a compacted gravel base covered with a thin layer of sand to provide a safe and solid foundation for stone steps.

◀ Broad steps of dry-laid stone are set into this steep slope.

Cost

Prices for ready-made stone steps vary greatly, depending on the type of stone and size. Stone steps are among the most expensive stone products sold. Flagstone steppers and traprock are relatively inexpensive and make safe steps.

Installation

Scale: 1 (least time and effort) to 5 (most time and effort).

■ Stone steps from ready-made steps: 2.

■ Stone steps from flagstone or other: 1.

For construction details, see *pages 136–137*.

INTRIGUING STEPS TO TAKE

If you think a pathway disappearing around a corner lends an air of mystery to the landscape, wait until you see and feel the effect caused by steps that vanish around a bend. What's up (or down) there? When designing a pathway across a slope, consider adding gentle curves that disappear around trees or shubs, then place your steps at the curves.

STAIRCASES

A stone staircase provides the best way to climb a steep slope. Staircases have a more formal look than random steps, and should always contain steps of uniform rise and tread. They usually have walls on each side of the steps to retain soil because of the excavation involved. Staircases fit the landscape best near the house or another structure. Formal staircases work well as entryways to raised patios, pool decks, or the front door of the house.

Staircases can be constructed from precut stone steps, wallstone, flagstone, or a combination of stone types. Mortared flagstone staircases are perhaps the most common stone steps.

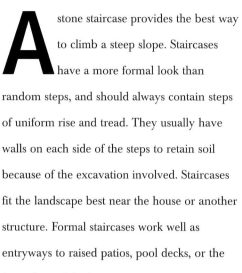

▲ This flagstone staircase combines with a low retaining wall to mark the front entryway.

Material characteristics

Stone suppliers sell thick slabs (4 to 8 inches) of stone that have been broken into widths suitable for staircases. Limestone, bluestone, sandstone, and granite steps for staircases are all commonly available in random lengths. Some stone yards will split steps to specific widths.

Stone steps are priced by the square foot of surface area or, in some regions, by weight. They are packed on pallets, one to four steps per pallet, depending on the step size.

Wallstone

Broad slabs of cut wallstone make attractive, uniform staircases. Wallstone is priced by the ton and packed on pallets.

Flagstone

Flagstone comes in large sheets $\frac{3}{4}$ inch to 4 inches thick. Quartz, granite,

▼ Level, smooth surfaces make safe steps. Height and depth should be the same for all steps to prevent trips and falls.

and limestone are common types of flagstone. Sheets can be as large as 40 inches across. Flagstone steppers are smaller pieces of flagstone, usually from 10 to 20 inches across. Flagstone colors vary widely, depending on the type of stone. Flagstone is sold by the ton and is transported on pallets.

Design and use

Staircases look more formal, so they serve best near the house. They can look out of place far off in the landscape. A staircase is ideal between the yard and a raised stone patio or where the contour of the land drops from the patio. Where a short, steep hill rises from the public sidewalk to the flat portion of the front yard, a stone

ACCENT STEPS WITH COLORS

For an eclectic look, use one color of flagstone for each step riser and a different color for the tread.

staircase is almost a necessity. To upgrade any concrete staircase poured when the home was built, replace it with stone.

Cost

Ready-made stone steps vary greatly in price, depending on the type of stone, but stone steps are among the most expensive stone products available. Flagstone and wallstone are relatively inexpensive and can be used for steps.

Installation

Scale: 1 (least time and effort) to 5 (most time and effort).

■ Stone staircases from ready-made steps: 2.

■ Stone staircases from wallstone: 3.

■ Mortared stone staircases from flagstone: 5.

For construction details, see *pages 136–137.*

◀ **Lighting highlights the staircase as a landscape feature and makes the steps safer at night.**

PATIOS AND OUTDOOR LIVING SPACES

▲ Widely spaced flagstones with grass growing between them create an area suitable for sitting or setting up tables for outdoor dining.

▲ A simple gravel patio with some chairs and potted plants makes a great garden getaway.

The reward for creating a beautiful landscape is taking some time to relax and enjoy it. And the best way to enjoy it is from a well-designed outdoor living space. An outdoor room, whether an elaborate outdoor kitchen or an intimate retreat, is most likely to be well used when it is convenient, comfortable, and reflects your family's lifestyle.

An outdoor living space should settle into a site rather than impose on it. Materials should blend into surroundings, making stone a good choice. Stone patios require little maintenance and last for many years. Choose materials and a style to blend in with and complement nearby plantings or structures, or contrast them.

When planning an outdoor room, consider the seasons and times of day you will use it. Observe sun and shade patterns and prevailing winds. The warmth of a southern exposure may be welcome on an early spring day or a crisp autumn morning, but it may make your outdoor room unusable on an August afternoon. Patios usually get the most use in the evening, so consider sites that will keep the setting sun out

◀ A flagstone patio with a stone-sided spa makes a relaxing outdoor sitting area.

of your eyes. If practical, consider wrapping your space around two sides of your house to take advantage of the movement of the sun and different views.

A logical location for a patio is through a door from the most used room in your home. However if you're looking for a quiet retreat, consider a small patio off your master bedroom, study, or home office. Outdoor sitting spaces are usually located in a garden, away from the daily bustle around the house.

Consider the functional aspects when building an outdoor living space too. The surface should be safe, durable, and well drained. If you live in areas of heavy rainfall, avoid materials that are slippery when wet. Make sure your plan provides adequate foundation and drainage; it's difficult to raise sunken flagstones back up to level and nobody likes to dodge puddles after every rain. If a stone surface will not be shaded, take steps to make it more comfortable for bare feet during the midday sun. Use rougher fieldstone, which reflects or retains less heat than cut stone, and pick a light color, which will absorb less heat than dark stone.

DINING AREAS

Dining areas range from an expansive patio with seating for 12 and a fully equipped outdoor kitchen to a quiet alcove in the garden with just enough room for a small table and two chairs. If your landscape allows for it, plan several dining areas that you can use at different times of day and for various types of entertaining.

Material characteristics

A major consideration when planning an outdoor living space is whether to mortar the stone or dry-lay it. Mortared cut stone is the most formal surface, and is level and safe. Other suitable surfaces include dry-laid cut stone, mortared flagstone, and dry-laid flagstone.

Limestone, sandstone, and slate are durable and attractive flagstones. Mortared flagstone's

▲ Dappled sun makes this flagstone patio a bright place for breakfast or lunch.

smooth surface is well suited for dining furniture. Use flagstones 1 to 2 inches thick, mortared to a poured concrete slab for stability and durability. Where winter temperatures dip below zero, the mortar will disintegrate over time, but not at a rate that makes this type of patio unsuitable in these areas.

Design and use

The size of your outdoor dining room depends on the number of people likely to occupy it at any time, the amount of furniture to be used in it, and the space needed for people to circulate. An advantage of outdoor dining is that overflow space (on the lawn and in the garden) is often close by. Advance planning can make the surrounding area available for overflow, so you can still have an annual party for 100 guests

▼ Stone adds character to this poolside outdoor kitchen.

▲ This southwestern courtyard is a great place for a dinner party or a casual family supper.

COOKOUTS BECOME MORE ELABORATE

Outdoor kitchens, the latest development in outdoor living, transform an ordinary cookout meal into entertainment. Usually an extravagant grill is at the center of one of these outdoor rooms. While not for everyone (some gas grills cost $2,000 or more), you may want to consider one if you enjoy cooking and entertaining. Constructing an outdoor kitchen is beyond the scope of this book, but several books about building outdoor kitchens are available, including *Better Homes & Gardens Outdoor Kitchens*.

and not have to build a patio to accommodate them all. (The photo on *page 52, top left*, shows one way to create a dedicated overflow area.) A solid, even surface is essential so furniture won't wobble and people carrying plates of food won't trip. The dining area should be close to the kitchen for easier serving and cleanup.

Stone for the surface should blend with your home's exterior and with the design and colors in the adjacent indoor room. If your dining area abuts a tiled floor, choose a stone that will blend with or complement the colors of the tile for continuity indoors to outdoors.

Cost

Flagstone falls into the upper-middle price range of materials suitable for an outdoor dining area. Cut stone is on the higher end.

Installation

Scale: 1 (least time and effort) to 5 (most time and effort).

■ Dry-laid dining area: 4.

■ Mortared dining area: 5.

For construction details, see *pages 138–141*.

◀ Dinner for two is a special delight at this intimate spot a few steps up from the garden.

SITTING AREAS

You can put an outdoor sitting area anywhere. The best locations are slightly secluded, such as a hidden spot at the end of a curving path, a quiet garden corner, or a sheltered place where you can enjoy a nearby pond or waterfall.

▲ This cozy corner surrounded by a stone wall and scenery invites restful pause and reflection any time of day.

Material characteristics

Because sitting spaces will probably handle less traffic and furniture than outdoor eating areas, they can be built of a wider range of materials. In addition to cut stone and flagstone listed in the dining areas section on *pages 54–55*, you could use fieldstone or cobblestone, both either mortared or unmortared. Gravel could also be used for an informal sitting and relaxation spot.

Design and use

Your sitting space should blend into the surrounding garden area or relate to any nearby building. Consider colors, styles, and textures of nearby buildings, choosing stone that will complement what is already there. If your sitting area is by itself, be creative; incorporate different materials of complementary or contrasting colors and textures. This space should be calming and relaxing, so avoid making it too busy or fussy.

PLANTING IN THE CRACKS

Planting moss or creeping plants in joints between stones adds style to a sitting area. Look for plants that can tolerate dry, hot conditions, such as lady's mantle, violets, and saxifrages. Creeping thyme, which gives off a fragrance when you brush against it, can withstand light foot traffic. Paving restricts plant competition, so once a plant is established, it will usually thrive without further attention.

▲ With a fence for privacy and a fountain to provide soothing sounds, this retreat is ideal for reading or an afternoon sunbath.

Site your outdoor sitting space in a secluded, comfortable spot that is sheltered from the wind and hot summer sun. Take advantage of a garden view or the sunrise or sunset. If your space will be used for entertaining, make it large enough for outdoor furniture, including armchairs and tables. Create a focal point for the area when possible. Consider decorating your outdoor space with a special urn filled with interesting or unique plants, a piece of sculpture, or even a reflecting pool.

If the best location for your outdoor lounge is in an open area, plant a hedge, put up screens or trellises with climbing plants, or build a fence to increase the feeling of intimacy and privacy. For permanent protection from the sun, build an arbor or pergola or plant trees to shade your space. A patio umbrella will give you shade instantly so you can relax until the trees provide shade.

▲ A bridge and a path lead to this sitting space, partially hidden behind shrubbery and tall plants.

Cost

Stone for sitting spaces ranges from gravel, the least expensive, to fieldstone and cobblestone in the middle price range, flagstone in the upper-middle bracket, and cut stone at the top.

Installation

Scale: 1 (least time and effort) to 5 (most time and effort).

■ Informal gravel space: 3.

■ Dry-laid stone: 4.

■ Mortared stone: 5.

For construction details, see *pages 138–142.*

CONTAINER SPACES

▲ A bench and a container of flowers make this a relaxing stopping point along a path, *above.* The gravel path, *opposite above,* widens at the curve to provide space for three containers.

something like a delicate piece of sculpture or expensive pottery, make the surface as flat as possible: Use cut stone instead of cobblestones or gravel, for example.

Design and use

Almost every sitting space or patio has a bench, and a container or two of showy annuals enhances any bench. Rather than taking up space on your patio for the container, buy some extra stone and bump out an area where you can place your container out of the traffic flow.

Incorporate your container spaces into your overall design and build them at the same time as the rest of your stonescape. You can add the containers at any time. It's usually best to use the same material as the adjoining patio or pathway. If you want to highlight the container or artwork, use a contrasting material. For example, a container space of colored gravel would contrast in both color and texture with a nearby sitting space made of neutral cut stone. Gravel is good for container spaces because it aids drainage.

A landscape is more than plants alone. Embellishments such as containers, sculptures, or whimsies are important elements. Instead of placing these as afterthoughts, enhance their impact by creating places where you can display these personal touches to their best effect.

Container spaces are specifically built to hold containers so they don't take up space on a patio or pathway, or in the garden. These spaces also can be built to highlight a sculpture.

Material characteristics

Any of the materials used for pathways or patios will make a container space; you just need to provide a relatively flat surface where you can set your container. If the space will display

Cost

A wide variety of materials is suitable for container spaces, so costs span the range of stone prices. To reduce the overall project cost, you can build container spaces of less-expensive

REACHING NEW HEIGHTS

A pillar is a variation on the container space. Often built to mark the entrance to a driveway or pathway, pillars can be placed anywhere you want to add interest. Top them off with annual-filled containers to bring color to eye level. Climbing or trailing plants are just right for pillar plantings too.

■ Stone pillars must pitch slightly inward toward the top. If the weight of the pillar doesn't push in upon itself, the pillar will probably topple over. A large, heavy capstone at the top also adds stability. A capstone gives a finished appearance and provides a perfect place for a container or statue.

material that complements the pathway or patio it adjoins. For example, place a flagstone or a few flagstone steppers next to a cut-stone path to make a container surface.

Installation

Scale: 1 (least time and effort) to 5 (most time and effort).

■ Dry-laid: 2.

■ Mortared: 3.

■ Pillar: 4.

For construction details, see *page 142*.

▼ A small stone surface that almost looks like some edging that fell over makes a spot for a container of colorful flowers in this garden.

Garden Edging

► Cut stone set into the ground makes neat, orderly edging for a garden.

E dging helps maintain the shape of a garden bed, prevents the soil from escaping, and helps keep grass from spreading into the bed. Garden edgings facilitate the flow of one surface into another, and often the edging material is purely functional and out of sight.

Garden edging can be decorative too, and it helps set garden style. A properly installed decorative stone edging will enhance almost any garden bed. Depending on the stone you choose and how you lay it, you can give your garden a relaxed, rustic feel or a formal, structured air.

If practical obtain samples of several edging materials so you can see how they look in your garden. Consider different ways of placing the stones for varied effects.

FIELDSTONE EDGING

Fieldstone edging gives gardens a casual, rustic look. These irregularly shaped stones come in

► Flagstone dug in on edge makes fence-like edging for this rose bed. The edging is set back from the lawn edge to make mowing easier.

many sizes and colors. Fieldstone edging reduces the formality of a geometric bed.

Material characteristics

Fieldstone is a naturally rounded stone, usually granite and usually collected from fields. It has an aged look and comes in random shapes, but at least one side is typically flat. Color varies greatly, ranging from dark gray to blue-gray, red, and even white.

Design and use

Fieldstone lends a rural appeal to the landscape and is an excellent edging for cottage-style gardens or informal mixed borders. A fieldstone border can be made more or less informal, depending on the way you face the stones' flat sides. Facing all the flat sides outward gives a more uniform, formal look. With the flat side in and the rounded faces out, the stones make a more rustic-looking border.

Cost

Fieldstone, available by the ton, is one of the least expensive types of stone.

Installation

Scale: 1 (least time and effort) to 5 (most time and effort).

■ Fieldstone edging: 1.

For construction details, see *page 142*.

▲ **Dry-laid like a low wall, flagstone edging curves along this bed for an informal look.**

DOUBLE-EDGED GARDEN?

Mowing a neat edge next to fieldstone-edged gardens can be a challenge. Some people install black plastic edging just outside the fieldstone as a second barrier. This creates an awkward space between the plastic and rock edgings where weeds can grow. It's usually best to skip the second edging and resolve to use a string trimmer after every couple of mowings. Another approach is to lay a band of gravel several inches wide between the lawn and garden bed. Plants at the front of the bed can grow over the gravel without requiring added maintenance. You'll have to keep the gravel out of the lawn, however.

TRAPROCK AND MIXED MATERIALS

▲ Traprock makes a rugged, solid-looking edge between this path and garden.

TRAPROCK EDGING

When fieldstone edging is a little too casual, use traprock. Much more angular and jagged than rounded fieldstone, traprock fits together more tightly, resulting in an almost solid edge.

Material characteristics

Traprock is a dark, extremely hard volcanic rock. Landscape pieces range in size from 10 to 18 inches across and weigh between 50 and 90 pounds. If you select your own stone, look for pieces that have at least one flat, or nearly flat, side. Color is a pleasing aspect of traprock: It reveals subtle highlights when wet, ranging from silver to deep purple.

Design and use

Traprock blends into a wide variety of landscapes, from country casual to urban formal. The irregularities of the stone keep it casual, but the elegant dark color gives it an air of formality.

Putting together a traprock edge is a lot like putting together the pieces of a jigsaw puzzle. With time you will develop a knack for selecting the right stones and fitting them together. Don't be impatient; if you are willing to devote the time, the result will be a handsome and long-lasting garden edging.

Cost

Traprock is economical. It is cost-effective for edging long beds or building raised beds (see the sidebar *below*).

Installation

Scale: 1 (least time and effort) to 5 (most time and effort).

■ Traprock edging: 4.

For construction details, see *page 142*.

RAISED GARDEN BEDS

Traprock can be stacked, an advantage it has over fieldstone. Unlike rounded fieldstone, the jagged faces of traprock make it possible to build a two-course wall up to about 18 inches tall. This is a plus if your bed runs along a gentle hillside and you need to make part of it a raised bed. For added stability use riprap (crushed traprock) to fill the areas between the two courses.

MIXED-MATERIAL EDGING

For a creative approach, compose garden edging of mixed materials. Materials can include different types of stone as well as other suitable materials or artifacts you find around the house or yard.

Material characteristics

Any of the stone materials described in this book can be used as a basis for a mixed-material edging. You can also incorporate brick, glass block, concrete pavers, wood, and metals into your edging.

Design and use

Depending on the materials you use in your edging, you can create any look, from urbane to rustic country. Traprock edging that includes glass block and wrought-iron pieces is best suited to a smaller urban garden. Fieldstone edging mixed with cut log ends and rusted metals looks better surrounding an informal garden in the country.

Cost

Cost of a mixed-material edging will vary widely, depending on the materials used.

Installation

Scale: 1 (least time and effort) to 5 (most time and effort).

■ Mixed-material edging: 3.

For construction details, see *page 142.*

CONTINUING THE THEME

Mixing materials in the edging is a step toward an eclectic garden look. To help the edging fit in, continue the theme throughout the garden. If your edging includes stone mixed with rusted metal, for example, carry the theme into the garden by placing larger metal items such as old farm equipment or old metal containers. If wood is part of your edging, consider a carved sculpture made by a local woodcarver.

▲ Stone pavers in the ground along the cut-stone path effectively set the garden apart.

ROCK GARDENS

▲ Low plants look best in an alpine-style rock garden on a gentle slope.

large gravel-covered slopes planted in dwarf conifers. A rock garden can solve landscaping problems. Sloping ground and hot, dry, windblown areas that present problems for formal landscaping are ideal places for rock gardens.

Natural stones already on your property usually work best in a rock garden. If there are no natural rocks, use a single type of rock from a local source. Rock from local sources looks natural for the area and usually costs less than rock brought from afar. Look for flatter stones rather than rounded boulders, and pick pieces in a range of sizes. Larger rocks have more impact, but they cost more and are harder to install, particularly because rocks look best when buried to two-thirds of their thickness.

A rock garden combines the strength and solidity of stone with the colors and textures of plants. This marriage of plants and stones evokes the feel of nature in ways other garden styles can't.

Inspired by distinctive plants in mountain settings, early rock gardeners attempted to replicate mountain scenes. Today the concept of rock gardening has expanded beyond alpine plants. Rock gardens now include small perennial beds enhanced with fieldstone and

Construction of a rock garden is usually more complicated than building other types of gardens. Place rocks properly the first time; moving large rocks is strenuous. Plan to have at least three people to help. Gloves and protective eyewear are essential. Think about rock placement in the planning stage and stand back often to view your work in progress to save both time and your back.

Alpine plants are the traditional heart of a rock garden. But you can establish a beautiful, low-maintenance garden with a few showy, easy-to-grow perennials, annuals, grasses, and even shrubs. Most alpine plants are tough and drought tolerant and come from places with extreme climates. They thrive in intense sunlight, thin soil, cold winters, and strong winds. Many of them show this adaptation with

◀ Outcroppings and gravel make a lovely site for colorful spring blossoms and low shrubs.

▼ A garden-scale model train with buildings and accessories makes this rock garden an animated world of its own.

profuse, tightly packed flowers nestled close to the leaves that are less likely to be windblown and shattered. Foliage is a beautiful silver, blue, or gray because of protective hair or wax on the leaf surface. Small, leathery leaves—often evergreen—collect as much sunlight as possible while resisting the drying of heat and wind. Choose plants with these characteristics to give your rock garden a natural look.

Rock gardening takes patience. Rocks require thoughtful placement for a natural look, and many rock-garden plants are slow growing. A rock garden mellows with age, becoming more enjoyable as the plants fill in around the rocks.

SLOPES, SLABS, AND SCREES

Slopes, slabs, and screes are three popular features for rock gardens. Any of them can be incorporated into a larger rock garden or serve as a complete rock garden by itself.

SLOPES

A slope is simply a rock garden set into a natural incline. You can install one anywhere there is a hill or berm of any size. A slope differs from a stone retaining wall in the spacing of the boulders; they are placed separately for a slope instead of being stacked together. Use one type of stone throughout the slope, varying the sizes. If the stone is grained, set each stone so the grain runs in the same direction for a more natural look.

▼ Boulders, low conifers, and shrubs stabilize and beautify this slope.

Material characteristics

Use stone native to your area, if possible.

Limestone, sandstone, and granite boulders are all suitable. These are usually sold by the ton.

Design and use

A slope resembles a natural outcropping with several stones. A slope retains soil like a retaining wall, but is usually more attractive than a boulder retaining wall. Build a retaining wall if the hill to be retained is steeper than 45 degrees because soil erosion will be difficult to control with a slope.

Grow plants throughout the slope, even on a mild incline, to halt erosion. Place the boulders and smaller stones so they create level pockets for soil. This will help the plants become established and reduce runoff when watering. A stone slope can fit into the landscape wherever there is an incline, whether it is beside the front porch or in a far corner of the yard.

Cost

Prices vary, depending on the type of stone. Boulders are usually the least expensive stone.

Installation

Scale: 1 (least time and effort) to 5 (most time and effort).

■ Slopes: 3.

For construction details, see *pages 143–144*.

◀ Pieces arranged to look like a stone that has broken up in nature are the centerpiece of this rock garden.

SLABS

A slab is an all-stone feature with pieces arranged to resemble a large, single outcropping that has split over time. Less dense stones, such as limestone, can be split along natural fractures into multiple slabs. Large pieces of granite may occasionally split along moisture-weakened seams. The stones are fitted back together during installation, leaving a gap of 1 to 10 inches between pieces. Stone suppliers often have presplit stones or will split stones for you.

Material characteristics

Stone available for slabs varies according to region. A stone may be split in two, or into as many as five sections. Split stones are sold by the ton and are delivered on pallets.

Design and use

Depending on the size, slabs create subtle to powerful focal points, and should be placed where they will be noticed. They look natural set into a flat expanse or a slope. For a great stone feature, locate three slabs where they are visible in one view, placing a midsize slab farthest from the house, a large one closer to the house, and a third, small slab next to the house.

▼ Stones spill from a gentle slope into this path, creating a rustic landscape.

SLOPES, SLABS, AND SCREES (CONTINUED)

▲ Larger shrubs and bushes accent this slope, making the smaller stones less prominent.

▲ The staircase in this slope fits well with the stones in the rock garden. Plantings visually link the stones on the slope.

Granite traprock (machine-split granite) can make an attractive, small slab. To create a traprock slab, pick out three, five, or seven stones of about 40 to 100 pounds each that seem to fit together. Vary their size. Test the stones for fit on the ground at the stone yard. You'll be surprised how closely you can match the rough, angular side of one piece with another so they look as if they were once part of the same large slab. A slab of seven or more stones should be at least twice as long as it is wide.

The gap between the stones in the slab can be planted. It's better to use low-growing plants so they will not hide the stone or your artful work.

Cost

Split stone slabs range from moderately expensive to very expensive. Stone dealers sometimes have naturally split rocks that were found on the ground as natural slabs. They are expensive but look best. Granite traprock is inexpensive.

Installation

Scale: 1 (least time and effort) to 5 (most time and effort).

■ Slab: 3

For construction details, see *page 144*.

SCREES

A scree is a prominent outcropping that is nearly all stone and resembles the stone piles found at the base of a cliff. A scree contains much more stone than a slope and has fewer, if any, plants. Instead of soil around the base of the boulders in a scree, crushed stone is used as mulch.

Material characteristics

Similar to slopes, see *page 66.*

Design and use

Construct a scree on a gentle slope. It will look best near the bottom of a long slope. The slope above the scree can be planted with evergreen trees and shrubs to accentuate the rugged, mountainous look.

Cost

Similar to slopes, see *page 66.*

Installation

Scale: 1 (least time and effort) to 5 (most time and effort).

■ Scree: 5.

Construction is similar to slopes, see *page 143.*

▶ Slabs of stone and gravel fill the space between this fence and the sidewalk, the kind of area that's often difficult to landscape well.

FOCUS ON PROPORTION

A rock garden, slope, slab, or scree must be in proper proportion to the whole landscape. It's difficult to set rules of scale (you know the proper scale when you see it) but as a general rule, don't think small. As much as two-thirds of the boulder might be underground, so get a large one. When laying out the project area, use a hose or rope to define the perimeter. Start out large; you can always make the outline smaller. If you start with a layout that's too small, you might not see a larger layout that could look even better.

▲ **Stones seem individually placed in this tranquil gravel garden.**

Gravel gardens, often raked with flowing patterns, have evolved from centuries-old Japanese gardens. This enchanting garden style adapts well to many landscapes. Gravel gardens today include large open floors with a few carefully placed rocks and shrubs, as well as casual cottage garden-like spots filled with self-seeding annuals. Creating a gravel garden is much like building a gravel path or patio.

Material characteristics

Gravel is made from crushed stone, usually granite. It's available in many colors with stone sizes from ⅛ inch to 1½ inches. To add another level of interest to your gravel garden, use several colors and stone sizes. Gravel also appeals to the sense of sound, crunching underfoot when you walk on it.

Design and use

A gravel garden is not only a place of beauty and serenity, it also requires little water, an important consideration for many areas of the country. A gravel garden is ideal for urban gardeners who have small courtyard gardens that are difficult to mow, or for homeowners who are away during parts of the summer and can't mow a lawn regularly.

Gravel gardens are not completely maintenance free, however. Gravel makes a great seedbed, so weeds can be a problem in a

▲ **Gravel flows among islands of bamboo and other plants in this garden. Flagstones create a platform for viewing and contemplation.**

◀ Carefully raked lines add motion and tie together the varied elements in this gravel garden.

gravel garden. Deadheading and careful plant selection will help prevent this. Gravel gardens that aren't next to a hard surface, such as a wall, will need a retaining edge. Also you will need to regularly remove gravel spillover from adjacent lawn or garden areas. Gravel sticks to shoes and is easily tracked indoors, so avoid placing gravel gardens right next to the house.

Cost

Gravel is relatively inexpensive and is sold in bags or in bulk (by the ton) at local garden centers and home stores. Buy in bulk if you are creating a gravel garden larger than 8 or 10 feet square.

Installation

Scale: 1 (least time and effort) to 5 (most time and effort).

■ Gravel gardens: 2.

PLANTS CAN GROW IN GRAVEL GARDENS

Gravel gardens can have greenery. After laying the gravel, top-dress the planting area with a layer of uniformly sized crushed gravel. Dig individual planting holes, and fill them with a mixture of topsoil and compost before planting. Areas not planted become paths. Gravel has a dry, Mediterranean look, so include plants associated with dry gardens, such as lavender, rosemary, thyme, artemisias, santolina, euphorbias, and lady's mantle, which tolerate shallow, well-drained soil.

OUTCROPPINGS AND ACCENTS

Outcroppings are boulders placed in the landscape so they appear untouched by time and human development. They are easy to install and have great impact. They're a focal point and can create a balance of color, form, and scale in the landscape. The boulders can be any size.

A stone outcropping serves well as the sole stone feature of a landscape, or it can be installed with other features. Adding a stone outcropping to any landscape makes the property look even more grand. Outcroppings

▲ Grasses and plants make this three-stone outcropping look like a natural part of the land.

work well anywhere, front yard or back. If you are building a home, have the builder set aside large boulders unearthed during excavation, then have the builder or landscaper arrange them on the grounds.

A stone feature sometimes creates the need for an outcropping: A flagstone pathway through the garden might look even more enchanting if there was stone nearby. Or stone garden edging might be enhanced by outcroppings throughout the garden bed.

The impact of a stone wall can extend beyond its immediate location when outcroppings of the same type of stone are placed a distance from the wall. Random outcroppings also can help secure the soil in a

▼ **Rising above the front garden, this distinctive stone is a landscape highlight.**

◀ The large stone is one of several strong elements in this section of the yard. Other stones have been placed near the steps.

berm or small hill, where a retaining wall would be too massive.

Accent stones are placed to look sculptural rather than natural. A boulder or boulders along the edge or the interior of a flagstone patio add stone accents. The flagstone is broken to fit around the base of the boulder. The boulder then becomes an accent, not an outcropping.

Stone can be sculpture too. A narrow, jagged 6-foot-tall piece of granite buried 2 feet deep in the yard, rising straight up from the grass lawn, adds a dramatic accent. Boulders with flat or slightly rounded tops become seats when placed along a pathway. A slab of limestone or granite set on boulder footings can make a marvelous bench. Used this way, the stones are functional accents, not outcroppings.

Stone supply yards often set aside particularly colorful, striped, or naturally weathered boulders to sell as accents. You can place one of these eye-catching, multicolored granite boulders in the center of a pathway so the pathway flows around the boulder on both sides, like water flowing past a rock in the center of a stream. Place small boulders of unusual shape or color in the garden bed for their ornamental beauty, or set them on metal stands, as you would gazing globes.

▼ Plants can grow on stones as well as between them.

OUTCROPPINGS

▲ Large stones mark the corner of this deck and serve as steps into the garden.

▲ This stone and the plants add a spot of color and texture to the garden.

Instead of just soil and plants as your landscaping elements, think of soil, plants, and stone. Outcroppings have a rugged, natural look and a sense of permanence unmatched by other stone features.

Material characteristics

Outcroppings can be boulders of any type. Granite fieldstone boulders are the most rounded, while granite traprock is jagged and multifaceted. Limestone and sandstone are often available as large, rough block shapes that can be stacked to form small cliffs. Wander through the stone yard when you're looking for an outcropping; you'll see many options.

Design and use

A stone outcropping can be the main focal point in the landscape or a secondary accent. Outcroppings look magnificent when placed so the entire stone is visible, but they also have a strong presence even when partially obscured by trees or shrubs.

Don't try to work out the placement of stone accents on paper. If you have drawn a landscape plan on paper, it may show where there is a gap between trees or a curving shrub or flower bed, both of which would be suitable for outcroppings. But designs often change at planting time. Outcroppings are best installed before the plants, so experiment with your plants while still in their containers, visualizing the outcroppings, until you're certain of your planting scheme. As planting continues, you may recognize places for outcroppings that you didn't see in your formal plan.

Outcroppings are relatively easy to place in an existing landscape. Study the photos in this book, then look across your yard. Walk the property so you see it from all angles. Visualize

outcroppings where there are bare spots lacking interest. Move a shrub if you think it occupies a spot where there should be an outcropping.

Single boulder outcroppings can look fine, but an outcropping consisting of a large, medium, and small boulder nestled together looks more natural. This rule of three also applies to three single boulders used as individual outcroppings: They can be spaced some distance apart, but if all three are visible in one view, the scene will appear complete.

Multiple outcroppings make a more natural display. Roughly balance the outcroppings throughout the landscape, while maintaining a random appearance.

Cost

Cost of stone used for outcroppings will vary widely, depending on the type of stone used.

Fieldstone boulders are the least expensive.

Installation

Scale: 1 (least time and effort) to 5 (most time and effort).

■ Outcroppings: 2.

For construction details, see *page 145*.

▲ Planting spots formed by accent stones dot this slope garden.

▼ Large stones mark the corner of this raised bed and form sides for the stairs.

ACCENTS

▼ This garden seat is a stone slab set on concrete bench legs. Twigs have been bent and lashed together to make the back.

The number of ways to use stone as accents is limited only by your imagination. As you begin to purchase and work with stone, you will develop a knack for stone construction along with an artistic sense and an ability to present stone in a variety of ways. Experiment; don't hesitate to express your taste and personality by creating unique stone accents.

▲ Stones that look like chairs are a fanciful addition to this yard.

Material characteristics

Stone of all types can be used to create landscape accents. Larger landscape supply yards often sell specialty or decorative stone varieties like these: *Calcite marble* is embedded with colored silicate. *Diopside* is quarried near rivers and often features crystal coursing and a glassy luster. *Hisingerite* has a shiny deep purple to black coating. *Fossilized rock* comes in a variety of subtle tones that deepen when wetted. Visit your local stone supply yard to see what types of stone catch your eye.

Design and use

Think of stone accents as garden sculpture, ornamental accessories, or furniture—perhaps a

combination of all three. Stone accents can be as subtle as a rounded yellowish fieldstone partially hidden by the deep green leaves of a hosta, or as bold as jagged granite boulders placed like islands in a sea of gravel. Brightly colored or uncommonly shaped stones and stone that has been polished or made porous by nature are particularly valued as stone accents. Combine a few distinctive stones with a piece of driftwood and perhaps an antique horseshoe to create a focal point for a table, deck, or patio. Or mark the entrance to a shady woodland pathway by placing light-colored stones to each side.

Stone accents can be functional pieces of art. Most visitors will admire—and sit upon—a bench made of stone. Stack flagstone to make pedestals for containers of blooming annuals. A chess-loving gardener can build a garden chessboard out of 24-inch squares of dark gray and silver quartzite, complete with stone chess pieces.

Recycled materials can make attractive accents. Find whimsical, creative uses for flagstone left over from a patio project, or wallstone pieces left over after the retaining wall is completed.

Cost

The price of stone used for accents varies greatly, depending on the size and type of stone.

◀ Stacked stones make a place to sit down or set a flower basket.

Specialty stone varieties described on the *opposite page* are in the moderate-to-expensive price range.

Installation

Scale: 1 (least time and effort) to 5 (most time and effort).

■ Stone accents: 1 to 5, depending on concept.

For construction details, see *page 145*.

ADD ACCENTS TO PROJECTS

Many stone projects can incorporate stone accents. A pattern of large fieldstones set into a dry-stacked wall of 1-inch bluestone adds artistic flair. Or place a single, large piece of flagstone in a sharply contrasting color in the center of a flagstone patio for decorative effect. Gravel pathways edged with cobblestone or flat, round river rock set on edge are classic examples of stone accents.

PLANTER BOXES

▼ This planter box and pergola create a classic patio style.

Stone planter boxes combine form with function in a colorful landscape feature that can be placed anywhere. Think of planter boxes as container gardening on its grandest scale.

Stone planter boxes are raised beds contained by stone. They can be round, oval, or have any number of sides to form any shape. L-shaped or quarter-circle boxes look terrific where the driveway meets the walkway leading to the front door. Rectangular planter boxes against an exterior wall of a house–often beneath a window–have long been popular, as have boxes that curve along the contours of a patio or pathway. Planters built against an exterior house wall can be three-sided, semicircular, or half-oval. A planter can divide one section of the yard from another. Anywhere you put one will add a rock-solid, colorful focal point to the yard.

Planters work well in pairs: Two stone planter boxes, one on each side of the driveway at the street, establish a grand entrance. Filled with colorful flowers, they offer a cheerful welcome to guests. Boxes at the driveway can have lighting and address numbers.

Square or rectangular boxes set near the house lend a formal look to the grounds, particularly when matching boxes flank the walkway or pathway leading to the front door. Line the sides of a dry-stacked stone planter box with landscape fabric,

then fill the box with potting soil. A mortared box should be smooth on the inside, but it does not need a liner. Colorful annuals will bring the box to life and provide season-long blooms. For a softer look on the side of the box, add trailing and vining plants along the edge. Perennials, bulbs, and even small trees and shrubs are all suitable for planter boxes, depending on the size of the box and the depth of the soil in it.

Planter boxes are great places to put plants in pots and other containers, especially houseplants in large pots or containers that you move outside for the summer. Build stone planter boxes for potted plants 8 to 12 inches deep on the inside. To adapt an existing deeper box for pots, put in a false floor of ½-inch pressure-treated plywood supported on bricks.

Plantings in stone planter boxes can change with the seasons. In the fall consider replacing ragged annuals with a fresh planting of colorful chrysanthemums. In northern regions evergreen garlands, cut stems of red-twigged dogwood, pussy willow, and spruce tips make a long-lasting display.

▲ **This complex planter combines circular steps with a wall and beds.**

▶ **This rustic planter provides plenty of seating.**

Material characteristics

Stone planter boxes, like walls, can be dry-stacked or mortared. Cut wallstone is a good choice for planter boxes. It stacks easily to create vertical sides, and the ends are easy to cut at angles to form curves. Flagstone, bluestone, cobblestone, granite pavers, and any stone suitable for constructing walls also may be used. Fieldstone is unstable when stacked, so it is less suitable; consider mortaring fieldstone boxes. Keep the size of the planter in proportion to its surroundings. Interior depth, which can be less than the overall height, should be adequate to hold enough soil for the plants you plan to grow.

Design and use

Consider the color and type of material used in the house exterior walls for stone planter boxes adjoining the house. This offers a great opportunity to create a contrast between the stone planter and exterior wall color.

The type of stone used to build the box can either match or contrast the stone used in other areas of the yard. It's best, though, if the stone used for the planter box is also used somewhere else in the landscape. Introducing too many types of stone into a landscape creates clutter.

Stone planter boxes can heighten and define patios. Build boxes on both sides of the patio entrance, or in each corner of a rectangular

▼ **A stepped wall connects this planter box to the house.**

STACK STONE FOR A PLANTER

Sometimes simple is best and quickest. You can create an artful, informal stone planter box in five minutes by simply stacking wallstone, cobblestone, or any other stone with relatively flat sides into a four-sided box rising a few feet above ground. You can use different types of stone left over from other projects. Don't score, saw, break, or cut anything. You don't have to line the sides with landscape fabric if the stones are set tightly enough together that soil won't run out cracks during heavy rain.

◀ Spaces between stones in this pond edging make small planters—more places for planting around the pond.

▼ A dry-laid planter box is relatively easy to build and becomes a point of interest in the garden.

patio. Consider placing one in the center of a large patio as a colorful hub. Stone planter boxes can be terraced and end in stone pillars to mark any kind of entrance.

Incorporate a sculpture or other piece of art into the box, and surround it with flowers. A small fountain or wooden tub containing water plants is effective when placed inside a box.

Cost

Cost of stone for stone planter boxes varies, depending on the type of stone used.

Installation

Scale: 1 (least time and effort) to 5 (most time and effort).

■ Stone planter boxes: 4.

For construction details, see *page 146*.

FOUNTAINS AND WATER BOWLS

Stone fountains and water bowls bring the soothing sight and sound of water to any setting. Fountains and water bowls take up less space than ponds, streams, or waterfalls, and are easier and less expensive to install. They are ideal water features for small gardens, patios, or courtyards. A fountain or water bowl makes an intriguing accent in a larger landscape too.

Home centers and landscape stores sell a variety of stone fountains. Depending on the design, stone fountains may spray streams of water into the air, bubble water through a hole in a stone or a pile of stones, or pour a stream of water into a bowl.

Fountains carved from stone are expensive, but their beauty and grandeur might make them worth the cost to you. Concrete fountains are now available that look like stone but are less expensive. They are perhaps the only concrete product suitable for use in a garden that has natural stone.

Water bowls

A water bowl is a traditional source of serenity and peace in a garden. This subtle, placid garden accent combines two basic elements, stone and water. Still water in the bowl reflects the sky; you can watch reflections of clouds passing by during the day and the stars at night. As water bowls have grown in popularity, stone supply yards and retail garden centers have added more sizes and styles of them.

Fountains

A fountain brings another dimension to your landscape: the sound of water. Whether it is the burble of water bubbling up through a hole in a stone or the splash of water falling from a spray plume, the soothing sound masks harsh outside noises, increasing your serenity. A fountain usually becomes the main landscape attraction, so consider location and size carefully.

◄ Water bubbles out through a hole in this stone, spills down the front, and is collected in a basin underneath to be pumped back through.

◀ Artifacts like this decorative urn are relatively easy to convert to fountains with self-contained pumps.

of these, a stone and pebble fountain is a simple, fun project you can do yourself (see *pages 147–148*). The fountain you make will be unique.

Concrete fountains made to look like stone are available in all styles. Concrete fountains are more affordable and can be beautiful, but even when wet, concrete does not have the same visual magic as stone.

▼ This carved stone basin is a pleasant surprise when visitors find it among the flowers.

Material characteristics

Stone fountains are made from every type of stone. Granite fountains are the most widely available because granite is quarried in many regions across North America. It is one of the densest stone types, unaffected by water running through it or across it. Granite also changes appearance greatly when wet, deepening the overall color while enhancing the various muted colors rippling through the rock.

Boulders predrilled for a fountain pipe are available at most stone supply yards in many sizes. Using one

FOUNTAINS

Design and use

Choose a fountain that matches the style and atmosphere of your garden.

Statuary fountains, commonly in the form of a human figure in the classic Greek style, add a dramatic element to both small and large landscapes. They work best in a pond, in formal or semiformal surroundings. They sometimes look oddly out of place in an informal, rambling cottage garden or stuck into an otherwise unassuming backyard landscape.

▼ A statuary fountain makes a commanding centerpiece in this garden.

▲ Water spouts through the center hole in this old millstone and runs into a basin beneath for recirculation. Stones on the face add interest.

Bowl fountains feature a central column with a fountainhead that sprays water upward to fall into one or more bowls on the column. Their strong symmetry gives them formality and calls for placement in a landscape based on orderly style and detailed design. Smaller bowl fountains are perfect for courtyards, cut-stone patios, and smaller garden rooms. Bowl fountains are best if you want a large, tall fountain. The largest fountains commonly sold at retail stand about 8 feet tall and have three or more bowls. Water overflows each bowl and splashes into the slightly larger bowl just below it. In a sheltered spot, this fountain can be heard even before it is seen.

Many stone fountains look less formal. Some resemble modern sculpture, with either rounded or extremely angular forms. These fountains, which vary in size, easily fit into any style of garden and landscape.

Large fountains look best with a backdrop of trees, shrubs, or taller perennials, including vining plants on walls and trellises. For a formal look, surround the fountain with plants.

All fountains require a water reservoir—a pool or pond—around the base, so remember to consider the space needed for the reservoir when choosing a fountain. The pool, an attractive water feature in itself, can be constructed with a formal or informal style and can have plants and fish, if you want. Shelter the fountain from the wind (or install a convenient switch to turn it off when the wind blows) to keep water from blowing away and emptying the pool on windy days.

Cost

The cost of stone fountains varies greatly, depending on the size and material used. High-quality concrete fountains that look like stone are usually less expensive than stone.

Installation

Scale: 1 (least time and effort) to 5 (most time and effort).

■ Stone fountains: Varies from 2 to 5, depending on size.

■ Boulder fountains: 2.

For construction details, see *pages 147–148*.

Also see pond construction on *pages 149–153*.

FOUNTAIN SHOULD LOOK GOOD OFF

Although the entire point of having a fountain on your property may be to experience the sight and sound of flowing water, there will be periods when the fountain is turned off (during winter in colder regions, for instance). Select a fountain that has strong sculptural qualities so it's attractive even when water isn't flowing.

▲ **A statuary fountain attracts attention in this garden pool.**

WATER BOWLS

The concept of the garden as a peaceful private sanctuary has inspired new interest in water bowls, subtle garden accents that have been used for centuries.

Material characteristics

Stone water bowls can be carved out of almost any kind of stone. Granite and marble bowls are best because the stone will not slowly absorb the water. Stone that has naturally formed into a bowl shape naturally is also available. These are usually kept in a special area at a stone supply yard.

Design and use

Depending on the size, a stone water bowl can be a small accessory, such as a bowl placed on a stone patio, or a major feature in itself, such as a large bowl centered in a large lawn.

■ Water bowls like the ones *above* and *below left* are often chiseled or sawn. You'll find them ready-made at larger stone supply yards.

You can tuck a water bowl carefully into a garden bed, where it may become partially obscured by foliage. A water bowl alongside a pathway invites guests to pause and enjoy the plantings nearby. Use them to accessorize decks, patios, stone walls, and steps.

Boulders that have large, concave dimples can be set as outcroppings, retaining water on their surfaces after a rain. Look for boulders like this when shopping at stone supply yards.

Remember that one of the best features of a water bowl is that it reflects what is above. A smooth water surface is enchanting in a woodland setting, where the tree canopy and patches of sky can reflect in the water. Colorful flowers next to a bowl reflect too. Place a water bowl beside a garden bench, where someone sitting on the bench can enjoy the reflection.

CARVE YOUR OWN BOWL

Carve your perfect water bowl out of stone. It doesn't take as long as you may think—perhaps as little as three hours. Here's how to do it.

■ Select a granite stone or boulder that has a flat or slightly concave side. Limestone and sandstone boulders work well also. Score the stone across the center using a circular saw with a diamond-tipped blade. Be sure to wear leather gloves, dust mask, and safety goggles. Set the saw's cutting depth to the desired bowl depth, and make the cut as long as the length of the bowl.

■ Next make a series of parallel saw cuts 1/4 inch apart on each side of the center cut. Make additional parallel cuts 1/4 inch apart for the width of the bowl. Make each cut shallower as you move toward the sides of the bowl. Because the saw blade is circular, the ends of the cuts will form the shape of the bowl.

■ Starting at one edge, knock out the big pieces of stone between the score lines with a 1-inch stone chisel and hand anvil. Work the chisel blade down and across the bottom of the bowl as you remove the stone.

■ Smooth the rough bottom of the bowl using a grinding wheel with a diamond-tipped blade. You can create a very smooth surface this way.

▲ **This sculptural water bowl looks right at home in a rustic cottage garden, but it would also fit into other styles.**

Butterflies might stop for a drink at a shallow bowl or one filled to the brim, and birds, of course, will probably drink and bathe there.

Water bowls require little upkeep. In hot, dry areas, water evaporates quickly so you'll have to fill the bowl often. Algae can grow in moist, hot areas, but a stiff brush will remove it. If birds frequently stop by, cleanup will be necessary.

Cost

Water bowls are usually quite affordable. Prices vary according to size and stone.

Installation

Scale: 1 (least time and effort) to 5 (most time and effort).

■ Water bowls: 1.

RUINS

ruin is a new feature built to look like an old stone structure. Ruins are often constructed to resemble parts of centuries-old stone buildings or walls that have crumbled with age.

The only reason for having a ruin within your landscape is sheer whimsy. In a rural setting, you might be able to convince visitors that a decrepit, overgrown fieldstone wall trailing off into the woods is several centuries old, but most often a ruin is built as a conversation piece or a visual delight.

■ The look of antiquity makes the garden *below left* and *right* intriguing to visit. Classic architecture and plants that seem to have overgrown the stonework add to the mystique.

Material characteristics

Any type of stone suitable for building a stone wall may be used for a ruin. If replicating a portion of a building, the walls of the ruin would be made in the same way and out of the same material as a stone wall. Fieldstone, flagstone, cobblestone, and bluestone are all good choices for constructing ruins.

Design and use

Ruins can be large or small, and can be constructed on any size property. A smaller site calls for a smaller ruin. A ruin should be set as far from the house as possible. In a large landscape, hide a ruin behind trees or over the rise of a hill where it will remain unseen until discovered.

A replica of the corner of an old stone house makes a great ruin. Dry-stacked flagstone or

bluestone works well for this project. Mortared cobblestone or fieldstone is another good choice. Apply the mortar unevenly so it looks like the mortar has crumbled away.

One wall may measure 8 feet long at the base, while the adjoining wall is only 5 feet long. Walls should be at least 18 inches thick—a typical wall thickness from centuries past. The walls may be 5 to 7 feet tall where they meet, with one wall a foot or so higher than the other. Wall height should trail off sharply as each wall runs away from the corner, replicating the way a wall would naturally disintegrate if neglected for years. (See the illustrations on *page 148.*)

SMALL RUINS HAVE IMPACT

Ruins can be small and still be effective. A broken stone statue can be a humorous ruin if a portion is still affixed to a precariously leaning pedestal while the rest appears to have tumbled into the hillside. A large clay pot laid on its side takes on added interest if half buried along the edge of a pond or bog, particularly as it slowly becomes covered in moss.

A remnant of a flagstone or cobblestone floor in the corner adds a nice touch, especially after weeds start to grow across it. And remember, in an actual ruin, the stone that was once part of the structure wouldn't completely disappear. Although some might have been carted off to build new walls, the rest would be scattered on the ground, with some pieces nearly buried.

Cost

Costs of ruins are similar to the the cost of stone walls of comparable size.

Installation

Scale: 1 (least time and effort) to 5 (most time and effort).

■ Ruins: Varies widely, from 2 to 4.

For construction details, see *page 148.*

◄ **This old well was already in the garden. With a new roof and cover, it becomes a real link to the past.**

PONDS

A water feature can easily become the highlight of a residential landscape. A pond or pool is the perfect project to start developing water attractions for your yard. (A pool is a man-made body of water that has neither fish nor plants.) Water, like stone, has captivated mankind since the earliest ages. A basic element, water is essential to all forms of life. Water and stone together in the landscape can create effects and moods ranging from soothing to spectacular.

Interest in water as a landscape design element exploded over the past decade as homeowners discovered the delights of having ponds, pools, streams, fountains, and other water features in the garden. Water features unlock new opportunities for gardeners, making it possible to add unusual new plants. You can even stock a pond with fish.

As interest has grown, advances in technology and marketing have made building ponds an economical, satisfying, do-it-yourself project. Pond kits featuring rigid, preformed, plastic tubs in a variety of shapes and sizes are an easy way to install a small pond. Larger ponds, and ponds of custom size, can be constructed easily using a rubber pond liner. In both instances stone is essential for building a rim around the pond to hide the edge of the tub or liner. Beyond that, stone can help you create a landscape around the pond that's either realistic or fantastic.

▶ The fountain in this pond helps aerate the water so it won't become stagnant. Water plants in the pond complete the water garden.

■ There's great pleasure in having a pond or pool close to a patio or other outdoor living area. The ones at *left* and *below* are carefully sited for maximum enjoyment.

Ponds fit any size property. A small container sitting on a deck can be a pond. With more space you can create a sprawling, natural-looking body of water that dominates the landscape. In all instances incorporating stone into the design creates a multidimensional, natural landscape feature.

Ponds and pools can be either formal or informal. Rectangular reflecting pools built by the Greeks centuries ago remain part of classic Italian and English garden design. Formal reflecting pools in manor gardens are large—some 100 feet long or more. On a smaller scale, reflecting pools have become popular in residential gardens. Cut stone and flagstone cut to form a straight edge along the rim are often used to build formal garden pools.

Even swimming pools can share the glory of stone in the landscape with breathtaking results. While not usually a practical do-it-yourself project, a swimming pool surrounded by a stone deck or more elaborate stonework can be built by a swimming pool contractor working with a landscape designer or contractor.

▲ Exotic plants and lush foliage make this pool seem like a tropical lagoon.

A pond is almost everyone's favorite landscape feature. Stone helps transform a hole full of water into a natural, tranquil oasis.

Material characteristics

Fieldstone, traprock, flagstone, cut stone, and boulders of limestone, sandstone, and other types are good choices for building ponds.

Pond construction begins with an excavation, then either a rigid plastic tub or flexible rubber liner is installed. Stone is placed along the edge of the pond to hide the liner edge. Stone can also be used to hide parts of the liner or tub underwater. Small stones, gravel, and sand are worked into the edging and under the water in a pond where you want a natural appearance.

Design and use

Proper placement of a pond is important. Moist, low-lying areas are natural spots for a pond, although you should be certain that the area drains well enough that heavy rains or spring thaws won't flood the pond. If you plan to grow plants in and around the pond, the area should receive sunlight for at least half the day, more for certain specialty water plants, such as lilies.

If you will have fish, locate the pond where it will get a half day of shade. If the pond is in full sun, build in some stone ledges to shade the fish. It's often said that a pond should not be placed under a tree because the leaves will fall into the water. In fact if there are trees anywhere in the vicinity, leaves and other debris will get into the pond anyway. You can

▲ Hidden away and surrounded by stone, this pond has an almost mystical quality.

quickly pick up surface debris every few days with a skim net. So if you'd like a shady, secret pond in the woods, go ahead and build it.

A common mistake in building a pond is making it too small. Building a pond takes considerable time and work. It takes twice the amount of work to tear it out and start over when you realize it should have been larger. The larger the surface area of the water and the greater the pond depth, the more options you have for plants and fish. Maintaining good water quality is also easier in a larger pond.

Cost

The cost of stone used in ponds varies, depending on the type of stone used.

Installation

Scale: 1 (least time and effort) to 5 (most time and effort).

■ Ponds: 4.

For construction details, see *pages 149–153*.

NATURAL OR ORNAMENTAL?

For a natural-looking pond, build it with stone native to your region. Don't mix stone types. Fieldstone naturally comes in different colors and is a good choice for pond edging. Cut stone is the perfect edging for formal rectangular or square reflecting pools. For an ornamental pond, consider raising the pond edge by installing concrete block above ground and facing it with mortared flagstone.

▶ **This swimming pool features plenty of flat rock surfaces for sunning and has broad stone steps into the water.**

STREAMS AND WATERFALLS

The sight and sound of running water bring life to a landscape. Running water in a garden can create feelings ranging from excitement to serenity, depending on the water feature's layout and design. The sound of even the smallest stream or waterfall will draw people toward it, even if it's not in clear sight.

The type of moving water suitable for a particular landscape depends on the scale and layout of the setting. Large country gardens can support streams and waterfalls of great size. A smaller suburban garden would probably be limited to a small but mesmerizing trickle of water, or water splashing over rocks to cool the garden in the summer months.

Any stream or waterfall adds a strong design element and point of interest to the garden. It's important to integrate the feature into the garden design, otherwise such a dominant element might overwhelm the rest of the landscape. You should match the scale, materials, and style with what is already in place. Or you can alter the existing landscape to accommodate a water feature.

The complementary characteristics of water and stone—water's movement and transparency, stone's repose and solidity—create a satisfying effect that can improve almost any landscape. Enhance the sound, and the pleasure, by incorporating stones that will cause water to splash or swirl as it flows around them.

Rocks also serve practical functions in a water feature. Large, flat rocks laid around the perimeter of a pond or pool conceal and protect

◀ **Large stones in this streambed divert water and cause it to splash, enlivening the sound.**

◀ Water flowing over large, flat stones creates a natural-looking waterfall. This type of waterfall works well with a pond, spa, or swimming pool.

the edges of the liner and form a transition to the surrounding landscape. When you want a path across a stream, firmly installed flat stones are your best bet. These carefully placed stones will also provide work platforms where you can perform maintenance. Careful selection of the lip rock the water flows over is key to making a natural-looking waterfall. Water falls over the edge of such stones, like those in the photo *above*, rather than trickling down the side.

As with pools and ponds, streams and waterfalls can be costly and labor-intensive to install and require ongoing maintenance. The water must be replenished frequently because of evaporation. Pump filters should be cleaned periodically, and

leaves and debris can collect in reservoir pools. Careful planning, design, and construction— sometimes with the help of a professional landscape designer or contractor for a complex installation—are the keys to having a successful stream or waterfall.

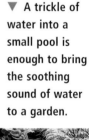

▼ A trickle of water into a small pool is enough to bring the soothing sound of water to a garden.

STREAMS

▲ Water splashing down a stone streambed is refreshing to see and relaxing to hear.

▶ A dry stream (see sidebar *opposite*) is easy to install and can improve drainage in the landscape.

Few homes can boast a natural stream or brook running through the property. But you can bring running water and its sounds to any landscape with a circulating pump. As they often do in nature, rocks play an important role in the beauty and impact of artificial streams.

Material characteristics

Hard and durable rock is best to use around water, especially moving water. Work with granite or other hard rock readily available in your region; it will be relatively inexpensive and will probably look more natural. Avoid limestone and sandstone–they will flake and deteriorate, leaving particles that can clog pump filters.

Design and use

Rocks serve several practical purposes in stream construction. Carefully placed large, flat stones conceal and protect the point where the liner meets the pool and make a smooth transition into the surrounding landscape. Smooth pebbles placed at the bottom of a stream conceal the liner entirely.

Rocks also improve the aesthetics of your stream and give it a natural look. Larger stones placed along the sides of your stream will provide a nice backdrop for plants and a place for frogs, turtles, and other aquatic life to bask.

A few carefully placed stones will divert a stream, producing interesting ripples and currents. For a natural look, bury one-third to two-thirds of each rock to settle it into the bank or streambed. Occasionally move one or two boulders to make subtle changes to the stream.

Locate your stream in an area with a change of grade from high to low. Ideally obstacles (rocks) will change the pace and direction of the water. Position rocks to help the water swirl and ripple, and create places for water to pool along the way. Line these small pools with gravel and edge them with water plants for a natural look.

Cost

A stream can be an expensive addition to the landscape. Even a short, simple stream can be a labor-intensive project, but it is not beyond the reach of many do-it-yourselfers. Because of the technical aspects of stream installation, it's better to consult an experienced landscape architect or contractor for advice on a complex project.

Installation

Scale: 1 (least time and effort) to 5 (most time and effort).

■ Streams: 5.

For construction details, see *pages 149–154.*

▼ A series of low, stairstep waterfalls like a mountain brook is an effective design for a stream on sloped ground or where you don't want a high waterfall.

TRY A STREAM MINUS WATER

If a stream isn't practical, a dry streambed made of various-sized smooth stones and gravel is an attractive alternative. It suggests water movement without water, a pump, and piping. A dry streambed also helps channel rainwater and runoff into planted areas. Further the effect of a true stream with reed-type plants along the edges and a few large, flat stepping-stones for crossing the stream. (For construction details, see *page 155.*)

WATERFALLS

The most dramatic features involving stone and water are waterfalls. Stones are the jumping-off points for water as it leaves one level and falls down to the next. The dramatic qualities of a waterfall depend on the height and slope of the stone the water tumbles over.

Material characteristics

In most cases the *lip stone*, the main stone the water pours over, should be fairly flat and larger than the other rocks around it. It must jut out past rocks below. Water falls best over a sharp edge, preferably with a slight undercut; it will just flow down the face of a rounded rock. Waterfalls must be built with hard and durable rock; native granites and other hard rocks are good choices. Limestone and sandstone will erode under flowing water and may crumble and flake off.

◀ Stacked stones at one side of a pond create an attractive waterfall even where there is no natural elevation change.

BAMBOO WATERFALL

Not every garden has room for a waterfall. You can get the look and sound of a waterfall from a bamboo fountain. This uses a recirculating pump to flow water through a bamboo stick into a stone container. Bamboo is not hollow, so you will need to drill through the corky membrane to insert plastic tubing. Some garden centers sell hollow bamboo especially for this type of project.

■ A high waterfall into a pool is dramatic. A lower, gentler one offers a fun place for smaller swimmers to play.

Design and use

The simplest waterfall is a single step, with water flowing from one level to another. Taller rocks stacked on each side of the waterfall channel the water, creating a sense that water eroded a gorge between them. A waterfall may also cascade dramatically in a dead fall of 3 feet or more. If your yard slopes steeply, take advantage of it and install a high waterfall, maybe with several pooling areas.

Most waterfalls are part of other water features, such as streams or ponds. Rocks in the waterfall should match those in the other projects. Select stones that will evoke the style you are looking for. Use taller, vertical rocks with strong texture to create the look of a mountain gorge and rounded, smooth stones for a gentle-terrained, lowland look. A few carefully placed stones at the base of the waterfall will cause the water to gurgle and foam, increasing the excitement.

Cost

Waterfall construction can be a major investment. It can be a substantial project for a do-it-yourselfer, depending on the design. It's advisable to consult an experienced landscape architect or contractor for a complex project.

Installation

Scale: 1 (least time and effort) to 5 (most time and effort).

 Waterfalls: 5.

For construction details, see *pages 149–154*.

CHAPTER HIGHLIGHTS

This chapter shows you the tools and equipment you'll need to complete stone projects. It also shows how to prepare your work site for a stone project, how to install base materials to ensure a long-lasting feature, and how to select, buy, and work with stone.

▷ You'll probably have to break some stone for any landscape project. This chapter shows breaking (see *page 123*) and other techniques you'll use to build stone landscape features.

STONEWORK TECHNIQUES

Working with stone can be an enjoyable and rewarding experience. Selecting stone, positioning it, altering its form when necessary, and ultimately creating a unique stone landscape feature brings not only permanent beauty (and greater value) to your home, but lasting satisfaction to you.

As you work with stone you will develop skills and gain knowledge handed down since ancient times. These skills and knowledge, along with modern tools and equipment and the wide variety of quarried stone available, will enable you to design and install the stonework projects featured in this book with the confidence that ensures success. The skills you'll learn are not difficult to master.

The following pages show recommended tools and how to use them, how to properly prepare the site, how to select and purchase stone, how to split stone and shape it in other ways, and most important, how to work safely.

When you start a stone project, take a little time to talk to the experts at a landscape stone supply yard. They have a wealth of knowledge and experience in selecting and installing stone.

Patience is important in any stone project. Working with stone is not a fast-paced activity. Haste can lead to injury. Always allow ample time for each project and be prepared for it to take longer. Learn to enjoy the relaxed pace as you develop these new skills.

TOOLS AND EQUIPMENT

Y ou probably already own some of the tools and safety gear necessary for stone projects. Additional tools shown are available at hardware stores, home centers, or landscape supply yards. You can rent power tools and machinery.

Safety equipment

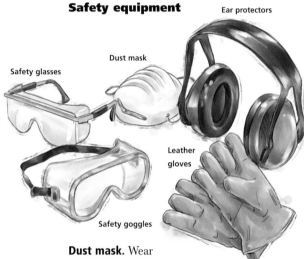

Ear protectors

Dust mask

Safety glasses

Leather gloves

Safety goggles

Dust mask. Wear a mask when dry or wet sawing, when mixing dry cement, or whenever raising dust.

Ear protectors or plugs. Wear when operating power tampers, saws, and skid steers. Headphone-type ear protectors muffle the sound better and are quicker to put on and take off than plugs.

Gloves. Wear gloves whenever you handle stone, use tools and equipment, mix concrete, or apply mortar. Good-quality leather gloves are best. Buy heavy-duty, rubberized work gloves for extensive concrete and mortar projects.

Goggles or safety glasses. Wear when chiseling, hammering, breaking, or altering the shape of stone. Also use when working with concrete and dry mortar to protect from splashes. Goggles offer the most protection.

Knee pads. Protect your knees by wearing pads when laying stone in the ground.

Leather work boots. Wear heavy boots, preferably with steel toes, every time you work with stone. Sandals, athletic shoes, or rubber gardening boots are not suitable for any work with stone.

Basic tools

Bow rake. Use a metal rake with a bow-like frame for leveling loose soil, sand, and gravel.

Carpenter's or mason's level. Check paved areas and walls with a level. You'll need two—one 1 foot long and one 4 or 6 feet long. A line level, which clips onto lines or cords to check their level, is also useful.

Mason's line. Use this twine for outlining project areas, measuring excavations, and establishing level when excavating slopes.

Garden hose. A hose is useful for outlining patios and pathways, or any curve in the landscape. Rope can also be used.

Measuring tape. A 25-foot steel-blade tape measure is best for most projects. A 100-foot steel tape measure is handy for laying out large projects, such as walls and streams.

Shovels and spades. A long-handled, round-nose shovel is best for general excavation of soil. Use a shorter, D-handled shovel for sand and gravel. A square-nose spade works best for cutting vertical edges and flat bottoms.

Straightedge. A perfectly straight 2×4 that's 8 or 10 feet long works well for making sure a large surface is flat. Use it also when measuring excavations or when determining grade for step projects.

Level with batter gauge attached

Levels

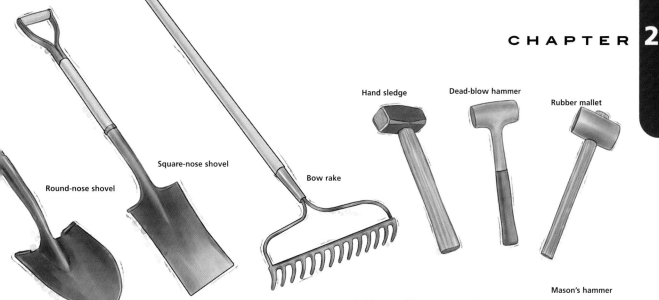

Hand sledge   Dead-blow hammer   Rubber mallet

Round-nose shovel   Square-nose shovel   Bow rake

Mason's hammer

Hydraulic splitter

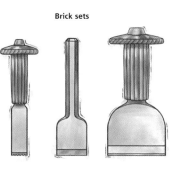

Brick sets

Tamper. This heavy, flat metal plate affixed to a stout handle is used for compacting soil and base materials.

Wheelbarrow. A metal wheelbarrow is the best choice for stonework. Plastic wheelbarrows are not as good for mixing concrete, and can split when used to carry stone and gravel.

Tools for breaking, trimming, and setting stone

Batter gauge. To maintain proper slope on the faces of walls, cut to the desired slope on one edge of a board that is the length of the level. Attach the board to the level (shown *opposite, top right*). When the level is plumb, the slope is correct.

Brick set. Used with a hand sledge, these blunt, steel chisels chip, trim, score, and break all types of stone.

Dead-blow hammer. This nonrebounding hammer with a hard plastic face is ideal for adjusting stone that has been placed and for driving smaller stone pieces into gaps in dry-stacked walls.

Hand sledge. Use this small, heavy, double-headed, steel hammer for breaking stone. You hold it with one hand.

Hydraulic splitter. Split quarried stone up to 8 inches thick with this heavy-duty hydraulic machine. Do not attempt to use it on rounded granite fieldstone. You can usually rent one from a contractor rental shop, although availability may vary by region.

Mason's hammer. This medium-weight hammer has both blunt and sharp ends for quickly chipping off bits of stone.

Portable dry saw. The diamond blade in this saw scores and cuts flagstone and scores other types of stone to facilitate breaking. It produces dense dust. You can rent one from a contractor rental shop.

Rubber mallet. Set and level flagstone and cut stone into sand or mortar with this hard rubber hammer.

Tools for mortar work

Mason's trowels. Apply and spread mortar in mortared stone projects with a mason's trowel. A broad trowel is best for carrying and applying mortar; a narrow one is handy for scraping away excess and filling small gaps.

Mortar box. This is a rectangular wooden box for mixing mortar. A steel wheelbarrow also works.

Mortar hoe. A mortar hoe has holes in the blade to efficiently mix mortar. A standard garden hoe will also do the job.

Sponge. Good-quality sponges of various sizes are used to wash moist mortar and bleed water from stone.

Wire brush. Used to clean dry mortar and crumbs from stone.

SITE PREPARATION

Before you can start laying stone for your project, you have to make the project site ready. Every project, from a garden path to a waterfall, begins with the following steps.

Locate utility lines

Call your local utility companies–gas, electricity, water, telephone, and cable TV–to have them mark underground utility lines on your property. It is crucial to know where these lines are, even if you are only excavating a few inches. Depths of the lines can vary. Many states offer a one-call service for utility marking; call the North American One Call Referral System at 888/258-0808. Ask to have the route and depth of each utility line marked. Also find and mark all sprinkler lines and outdoor lighting wires, if you have those.

Vegetation removal

Clear the project area of all weeds, including a space of several feet around the project. It is important that all perennial weeds and their roots be removed, particularly in pathway excavations of less than 4 inches. You can either spray the area with a glyphosate-based weed killer a week before starting the project, or simply clear away the weeds by slicing off and removing the top 2 inches of soil. Do this by digging with a square-nose shovel held nearly horizontally. If there are few weeds, water the area, then pull them by hand.

Cut down trees in the way. Call a professional tree service to deal with large trees. The stump and major roots must be removed during excavation for any tree that was growing in the project area. This is especially important when installing mortared pathways, patios, and walls.

The amount of time spent clearing the project area of vegetation depends on the nature of the project, and what's growing in the area.

Grading and drainage

You have to consider drainage any time the landscape is altered. Rain or moisture from a sprinkler will soak through a flagstone path set on a few inches of compacted base material and an inch of sand slower than it soaked into the same ground before the path was laid. Moisture will not soak down through a mortared stone patio or pathway at all. Such features installed in low-lying areas where the soil contains clay or otherwise does not drain well may be prone to flooding. Installation of perforated drainpipe

◀ The yard was cleared before construction started on this extensive stone garden. A clear working area makes the job easier and safer.

is one solution for potential drainage problems in poorly draining soils (see *page 115*).

If your soil drains normally and the patio, pathway, or other stone surface, mortared or not, is generally on the same grade as its surroundings, you should not encounter problems with excess moisture.

Where patios or other large stone surfaces are installed against or near the house, you should grade at least one-third of the ground next to the new stone area so it gradually slopes down and away from the house and stone

surface. Build the patio at or above the existing grade surrounding the house. Grading, if necessary, should be done before the project is laid out and excavated.

LAYOUT AND EXCAVATION TECHNIQUES

Garden hose and rope are the best tools for laying out curving pathways, patios, walls, garden edging, seating and container spaces, ponds, and streams. Rubber hose works best because plastic hose tends to retain its coil when you lay it out. Lengths of ½- to 1-inch-diameter rope work just as well if the rope remains completely limp after uncoiling.

To lay out straight lines and 90-degree angles, stretch plastic cord or string taut between wooden stakes. A taut line will mark a perfectly straight line between any two points in the yard. Cord and stakes with a line level are also useful if you need to find or maintain true level when working on a slope. Sidewalks, formal pathways, steps, walls, and patios all require establishing straight and level lines. You can lay out perfect 90-degree corners easily using batterboards and mason's lines, as shown on *page 108*.

Laying out pathways

Lay out curved pathways with two hoses. Measure from your design plan or determine the best route for the pathway by looking at the site. Then lay out a hose to represent one edge of the path. Move the hose around to give your pathway the curves you want. Once the hose is in place, lay out another one parallel to the first, placing them the same distance apart as the width of your path (see illustrations *below*). Ropes may be used in the same way.

For straight pathways or sidewalks, use wooden stakes and plastic cord. Buy wooden stakes or cut 12-inch pieces of 1×1 or 1×2 lumber and make a point on one end to drive into the ground. Wooden dowels or bamboo

LAYING OUT A CURVED PATHWAY

Use a rubber garden hose or thick rope to lay out curved pathways. You'll get a clear look at how the shape of the pathway fits with the landscape.

Lay a second hose for the path's other edge. Sticks cut to the width of the path and placed between the hoses keep the path sides parallel.

garden stakes will also work if they are stout enough to withstand the cord's tension. Pound the stakes 8 inches into the ground, then tie the cord to the first stake about 3 inches above the ground. Walk the cord to the next stake, loop it around, and pull the cord tight. Loop the cord around the stake several more times and tie it.

The illustrations *below* show the stakes and cords for layout of a straight, cut-stone sidewalk coming from the front door, then turning 90 degrees and running to the driveway. The sidewalk will run parallel to the house, so a tape measure is all that is needed to set the stakes and cords. To check that corners are 90 degrees, use the 3-4-5 triangle method described on *page 108.*

Laying out freestanding and retaining Walls

For straight freestanding walls, use the stake-and-cord method. For curved freestanding walls, use hose or rope. Measure with a tape measure to ensure that the cords or hoses are parallel. The distance between the cords or hoses will be the width of the wall at the base.

For straight retaining walls, stretch a single cord along the base of the slope to be retained. Place it the same distance from the slope as the thickness of the wall. For curved retaining walls, lay a single hose or rope parallel to the base of the slope at the same distance from the slope as the thickness of the wall.

LAYING OUT STRAIGHT LINES

Cord stretched taut between stakes always shows a true straight line. A tough nylon or nylon-blend cord with a bit of stretch works best.

Measuring the distance from the house to the cord and from cord to cord at different points ensures that lines are parallel.

LAYOUT AND PATIOS, PLANTERS, AND EDGING

When laying out a square or rectangular patio, employ a slightly more sophisticated version of the stake-and-cord system described on the previous pages. Instead of plain stakes, set up batterboards, which are easy to build and use. Batterboards work well for laying out 90-degree corners in large areas.

Make batterboards out of 1×2 or 2×4 lumber. Cut the 24 pieces 14 inches long to make four sets of batterboards. Cut a point on one end of 16 of the pieces.

Nail or screw the stakes together to make batterboards as shown at *left*. Assemble two pointed stakes with one plain piece across the top as a crossbar. Place the crossbar 1 inch below the flat tops of the stakes. Make two batterboards for each corner. Lay out the patio with a tape measure. Starting at one corner, pound a single stake into the ground at each corner. Then drive one set of batterboards into the ground about 6 inches outside each corner stake. Remove the single stakes. The crossbar ends need not touch, and are not attached to each other in any way.

Pound a small nail into the top horizontal stake of each batterboard at the point where it aligns with the true dimensions of the area. Tie a mason's line (strong cord) to the nail in one crossbar and cinch it up tight around the base of the nail in the batterboard at the opposite end. Set all four mason's lines. Check the four corners of the patio to see that each is a true 90-degree angle.

To check a corner for square, measure along one line 3 feet from the intersection of the two lines and mark it with a felt-tip pen. Mark the other line 4 feet from the corner, as shown in the illustration at *left*. Measure the distance between the marks. If the distance is 5 feet, the corner is square. If not adjust the lines by moving the nails along the crossbars. Confirm that all corners are true by measuring the distance between diagonal corners. The measurements should be the same.

LAYING OUT A SQUARE OR RECTANGULAR PATIO

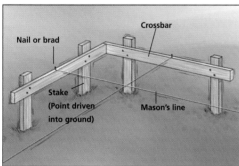

Mason's lines

batterboards

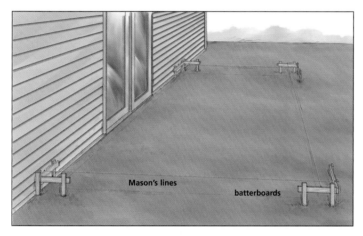

Crossbar

Nail or brad

Stake (Point driven into ground)

Mason's line

Use batterboards and mason's lines to lay out any square or rectangular area. Set batterboards 6 inches outside the area to be excavated.

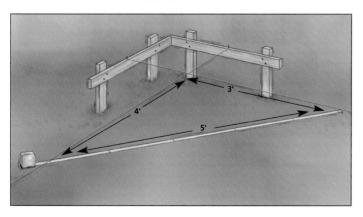

3'

4'

5'

Make a mark 3 feet from the corner on one line and 4 feet from corner on the second line. To square the corner, adjust the lines until the distance between the marks is 5 feet.

Laying out a curved patio or other curved space

Use garden hose or rope to lay out curved patios, seating areas, and container spaces. A hose or rope outline allows you to see the exact size and shape of the patio before excavation begins. The patio often looks different outlined by hose in your yard than it does as lines on paper. You can modify the size or shape of the stone patio as you mark it out with hose. Some professional landscape designers lay out a patio area on-site with garden hose before they draw it on paper.

Laying out stone planters

Stone planters with straight sides can be laid out with cord and stakes. If you want the box to be a perfect square or rectangle, use batterboards and mason's lines in the same way as a rectangular patio.

Laying out a garden bed and edging

Use garden hose or rope to define the edge of these projects. Don't overdo the curves; two or three graceful curves in a 25-foot garden bed look more natural than four or five.

LAYING OUT A CURVED PATIO

Use a rubber garden hose or rope to lay out a curved patio. A few broad, sweeping curves serve best.

LAYING OUT STONE PLANTERS

These layouts for stone planter boxes flanking a walkway are determined by the walkway, stakes, and cords.

EXCAVATION TECHNIQUES

With the layout complete, you are ready to excavate for the project. The most important goals in excavating are to keep the edge or edges of the hole true to your design layout and to maintain a uniform, proper depth throughout the excavation.

Marking the outline

Hoses or ropes can move or get in your way as you dig. If you outlined the edge of your pathway, curving patio, water feature, or other stone project this way, mark the outline for the project right on the ground, then remove the hoses or ropes. Here's how to mark them with spray paint: Hold the spray can only an inch or so above the ground and spray a narrow, continuous line of paint just inside the hose or rope.

You can also mark the lines with flour poured through a funnel or from a rolled-up sheet of heavy paper. Mark the lines with flour only if you are going to start digging immediately; a flour line will diminish within days and disappear in a rainstorm. Spray paint will last several weeks on a lawn or low-growing vegetation. Once the paint or flour lines are marked, remove the hoses or ropes.

If you marked the project layout with mason's lines or string stretched taut between stakes, you can leave them in place while you excavate.

Cutting the edge

Begin by cutting in the outline edges with a square-nose shovel. Stand on the outside of the paint, flour, or string line and face the excavation area as you move along the edge. If edging a project defined by paint or flour, cut just to the *outside* of the marking. If edging a project defined by mason's lines or string, place the shovel blade and handle on the *inside* of the string, then look straight down on the string to be sure you are following its outline.

RECOMMENDED EXCAVATION DEPTHS BY PLANT HARDINESS ZONES

	USDA Plant Hardiness Zones				
	2/3	4/5	6	7/8	9/10
Dry-Laid Patio	8"	8"	6"	6"	6"
Mortared Patio	10"	10"	8"	8"	8"
Dry-Laid Pathway	8"	8"	4"	4"	4"
Mortared Pathway	10"	10"	10"	8"	8"
Gravel Pathway	5"	4"	4"	3"	3"
Dry-Stack Walls	12-18"*	12-18"*	10"	8"	6"
Mortared Walls	50"**	42"**	20"	20"	20"

* Walls 1–3' high, 12–14" excavation; Walls higher than 3', 18" excavation

** Depth for frost footings. Installation by professional contractor recommended.

Dig the blade straight down into the ground to make a clean, straight cut into the ground. Drive the shovel into the soil as deep as possible. Push the handle forcefully away from you, moving the soil away from the edge. Remove the blade and continue along the marked edge.

Rough excavation

After you have cut the outline edge, switch to a long-handled, round-nose shovel and start removing the soil, beginning at an edge. The best method is to dig down in one smaller area until you are within about an inch of the final depth, then remove soil from the rest of the project area, maintaining that approximate depth. Don't dig to the final depth yet.

Measuring depth

Measure the depth of your excavation early and often. For proper depths, refer to the chart on the *opposite page.* The illustration *below* shows a way to measure the depth of a narrow excavation for a project like a pathway or planter. The way to measure the depth of a patio or other large excavation is shown on *pages 112–113.*

Finished excavation

After completing the rough excavation, switch back to the square-nose shovel. Hold it nearly horizontal to the ground and slide it forward, slicing a flat and uniform bottom to the excavation. Check again for proper depth throughout the area, and use the shovel to shave off any high spots in the excavation floor. You can leave the low spots; the base material will fill them. Straighten and clean up the vertical sides of the excavation.

To measure the depth of a pathway, wall, or other narrow excavation, span the excavation with a straight board, then measure from the bottom of the board to the bottom of your excavation. If you can find a perfectly straight 2×4 that's 10 feet long or longer, you can use it to measure wider excavations.

EXCAVATING FOR PATIOS AND PLANTING BEDS

Concern for tree roots

You'll probably run into tree roots, from small to large, running through the excavation area. They could be roots of nearby trees or of trees growing 50 feet or more from the excavation area. When installing a patio, you should remove these roots as you excavate, particularly if they are growing at or near the soil surface. Allowed to remain, tree roots will usually disrupt the level surface of a patio within a few years. Eventually they nearly always will disrupt and crack the mortar between the stones in a mortared patio or path.

Consider how chopping and digging these roots will affect the tree. The distance of the tree from the excavation site is one important factor. If the tree is 20 feet or more away, there will usually be few roots and they will not be large; removal should not hurt the tree. Trees closer to the excavation site, however, could suffer severe stress and even die from cutting or removing roots. You may need to consider a different location for the patio to avoid risking the health of the tree. Consult an arborist or landscape professional if you are in doubt.

Measuring depth

As you begin final excavation, add more stakes and lines across the area, as shown in the illustration *below*. Ensure that all lines are level by using a clip-on line level or by holding a standard level steady just beneath each line. All lines should be set a uniform distance—3 inches is good—above grade.

Measure down from the lines at points throughout the excavation to check depth. Figure the distance from the line to grade in your measurement. For instance if all lines run

RECTANGULAR PATIO

Add a line down the center of the patio and additional lines to form a grid of about 5-foot squares so you can measure throughout the project area. Be sure all lines are level.

3 inches above grade and you want a uniform 6-inch excavation, the floor of the finished excavation should be 9 inches from the lines.

Excavating a rectangular or square patio

Excavate a square or rectangular patio by cutting the edge and digging the rough and finished excavations. Follow the instructions on *pages 110–111* and refer to the excavation depth chart on *page 110*. Measure the excavation depth as shown in the illustration *opposite*.

Excavating a curved patio

Excavate a curved patio by cutting the edge and digging the rough and finished excavations. Follow the instructions on *pages 110–111* and refer to the excavation depth chart on *page 110*. Measure the excavation depth as shown in the illustration *top right*.

Excavating for stone planters

Excavate for stone planters by cutting the outside edge, then digging the rough excavation and the finished excavation to match the wall base thickness (see *pages 134–135*). Follow the instructions on *pages 110–111* and refer to the excavation depth chart on *page 110*. Excavate to the depth shown for the type of walls you will build. Measure depth as shown on *page 111*.

Excavating for stone garden edging

No real excavation is necessary to edge a garden bed with a single course of stone. Loosen the soil along the edge of the bed with a spade or tiller so the base of each stone can be set a few inches below the soil surface.

CURVED PATIO

Place stakes outside a curved patio excavation and run lines from the stakes to form a 5-foot grid across the excavation area. Measure down from the lines to check excavation depth.

STONE PLANTERS

Excavate only for the walls when constructing stone planter boxes. Soil can remain in the middle because it will be amended and tilled to form the soil in the raised bed.

INSTALLING BASE MATERIALS

After excavating, install the base material. Proper installation of base materials ensures long-term stability and beauty of any stone project. The chart below shows recommended base thicknesses. A variety of materials may be used:

■ **Crushed limestone.** Crushed limestone gravel with *fines*–small pieces and powder.

■ **Crushed granite.** Denser than crushed limestone, otherwise similar.

■ **Crushed concrete.** A good base material made from recycled concrete.

■ **Coarse sand.** A 1- to 2-inch layer goes on top of the base, except in mortared projects.

■ **Poured concrete.** Always the base for mortared stone patios, pathways, and walls. Use for tall dry-stack walls in colder climates.

RECOMMENDED BASE DEPTHS ACCORDING TO USDA ZONES

USDA ZONES	2/3	4/5	6	7/8	9/10
Dry-Laid Patio	6" compacted gravel	6" compacted gravel	4" compacted gravel	4" compacted gravel	4" compacted gravel
	1" sand	1" sand	1" sand	1" sand	1" sand
Mortared Patio	4" compacted gravel	4" compacted gravel	2" compacted gravel	2" compacted gravel	2" compacted gravel
	4" poured concrete	4" poured concrete	4" poured concrete	4" poured concrete	4" poured concrete
Dry-Laid Pathway	6" compacted gravel	6" compacted gravel	4" compacted gravel	4" compacted gravel	4" compacted gravel
	1" sand	1" sand	1" sand	1" sand	1" sand
Mortared Pathway	4" compacted gravel	4" compacted gravel	2" compacted gravel	2" compacted gravel	2" compacted gravel
	4" poured concrete	4" poured concrete	4" poured concrete	4" poured concrete	4" poured concrete
Gravel Pathway	3" compacted gravel	3" compacted gravel	2" compacted gravel	2" compacted gravel	2" compacted gravel
	2" finish gravel	2" finish gravel	2" finish gravel	2" finish gravel	2" finish gravel
Dry-Stack Walls	6–12" compacted gravel*	6–12" compacted gravel*	6–12" compacted gravel*	6–12" compacted gravel*	6–12" compacted gravel*
	1" sand	1" sand	1" sand	1" sand	1" sand
Mortared Walls	Professional contractor	Professional contractor	6" compacted gravel	6" compacted gravel	6" compacted gravel
	6–12" poured concrete**	6–12" poured concrete**	6–12" poured concrete**	6–12" poured concrete**	6–12" poured concrete**

* 6" compacted gravel, 1–3' walls; 8" compacted gravel, 4' walls; 12" compacted gravel, over 4' walls.

** 6" poured concrete, 1–2' walls; 8" poured concrete, 3' walls; 12" poured concrete, over 4' walls.

Compacted gravel includes crushed granite, crushed limestone, and crushed concrete.

TAMPING THE BASE

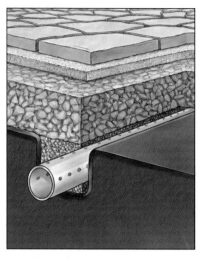

A hand tamper works well for smaller jobs, such as pathways. Tamp the area as firmly as possible, take a break, then tamp the area a second time.

A gasoline-powered plate compactor is best for large areas. Rent one with both forward and reverse. Start along the perimeter, then circle to the center. Compact base material twice.

Install a perforated drainpipe if drainage is a concern. Set the pipe at a slight downward angle away from the project area. Put landscape fabric on top of the pipe and cover it with base material to prevent clogging the side holes.

Compacting base material

Compact crushed gravel or crushed granite in 2-inch layers. Shovel the material in and distribute it evenly to a depth of 2 inches. Spread and smooth it with a bow rake. Rake with the tines down to pull and distribute the base material; turn the tines up to smooth. Compact this initial layer, using either a hand or power tamper. Add base material and compact each 2-inch layer.

Installing concrete base

Have a contractor pour a concrete base or do it yourself. If you do the work yourself, rent a portable mixer or have a concrete truck deliver it. Concrete bases must have steel reinforcement bars (rebar) or some other reinforcement. Refer to a book about concrete and masonry for more information about concrete work.

INSTALLING EDGING

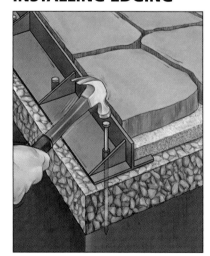

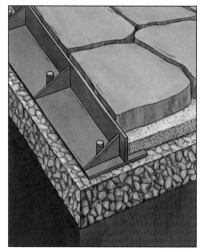

Use flexible plastic paver edging instead of wood to edge stone patios or pathways. Place edging on top of the compacted base material and secure it with 10-inch spikes.

Smooth a layer of sand on top of the compacted base and the inner base lip of the plastic edging. Adjust the height of the sand layer so the stone sits just above the top edge of the edging.

Selecting and Purchasing Stone

The first visit to the stone and landscape supply yard can be surprising. Stone and aggregate supply is a big industry, and there's an amazing variety of stone available to the consumer. The next six pages will help familiarize you with stone supply yards so you can choose and purchase stone wisely.

Visit more than one stone supply yard if there are several in your area. As with other retail businesses, not every supplier carries the same products. The largest supplier may have the widest overall range of stone, tools, rental equipment, and related products, but a smaller yard might carry flagstone in a particular hue not found anywhere else.

Wear casual clothes and work boots, and bring along a pair of tough leather gloves. Shopping for stone can be a hands-on activity. A notebook, tape measure, and camera are useful during preliminary shopping visits. If you are working from a design plan, bring a copy. Don't bring small children, if at all possible. A busy stone yard is a whirlwind of activity and keeping your children safe will take up most of your time. Pickup trucks, trailers, dump trucks, forklifts, skid loaders, and other heavy equipment operate among pallets of stone and mountains of sand, decorative rock, black dirt, and mulch.

Explain your project at the customer service desk and ask for a salesperson to show you the yard. Many stone yards are so large you'll need a salesperson to help you find what you're looking for. A good salesperson can also explain options and alternatives. Get a copy of the catalog, if there is one.

Selecting Stone
Shop when the sun is shining so you can see the truest colors in the stone. Ask where the various stones are from, what's on sale, and what's new.

Much of the cost of stone is for trucking the stone from the quarry to the stone yard. If local stone is available, it usually costs less. Here are other factors to consider when selecting from the basic stone types:

Flagstone. Flagstone (and flagstone steppers) must be thick enough for your project. For dry-laid flagstone pathways, patios, or seating areas, get stone at least 1 inch thick. Thicker stone is more stable and less affected by traffic. Use

▼ **A large stone yard will have many kinds of stone available in many forms. Ask for help if you are not sure what you need.**

flagstone less than 1 inch thick only in mortared projects. Choose flagstone with a smooth, even surface for patios and primary pathways.

Cut Stone. Cut stone for paved areas is usually less than 1 inch thick, intended for mortared installation. Cut stone for an unmortared pathway or patio should be 1½ inches thick to ensure against eventual cracking.

Quarried Wallstone. You'll find wallstone in a wide range of thicknesses, widths, and lengths. Thickness of individual wallstone pieces can

vary as much as 3 inches per pallet. This variance can make it difficult to lay a level, uniform top course on a low wall. If your wall will have only two or three courses, ask if the stone yard can deliver wallstone of a particular uniform thickness.

Boulders, Fieldstone, and Riprap. These materials are usually in large piles, sorted by size. They are sold in bulk, so you'll need to figure the volume or tonnage you need.

Figuring stone quantity

Stone and aggregate are sold by the ton, so you'll have to figure the tonnage you need for a project. You don't want to pay for delivery and unloading only to discover you didn't order enough. Computing stone quantities is not an exact science. You will inevitably have some amount of wasted stone and rubble with stone paving and some wall projects. Allow for 5 to 10 percent extra when figuring stone quantity. Here is how to figure correct stone quantities:

Flagstone and Cut Stone. All you need to know is the square footage of the project surface area. Salespeople at the stone yard will know how many square feet 1 ton of the flagstones and cut stones will cover. To figure the area of your 12×18-foot rectangular patio, multiply 12 by 18 to get a total of 216 square feet. If you use 1½-inch-thick Colorado red sandstone, for instance, the salesperson or catalog may tell you that it covers 90 square feet per ton. Allowing

for 5 percent waste, you would need to order enough for about 225 square feet, or 2.5 tons (225/90=2.5), to cover your patio.

Figure pathways, seating spaces, or any surface you are paving with stone the same way: Know the total square footage for the project area, and order accordingly.

■ Base materials and aggregates are sold in bulk. For a small to medium project, you can carry the material in a pickup. It may be more economical to have larger quantities delivered.

◀ Stone comes in a wide variety of shapes, sizes, and colors. When you shop for stone, explain your project so the salesperson can show you the best materials to use.

Quarried Wallstone. The amount of wallstone needed is computed the same way, except you need to estimate the square footage of a stone wall face, instead of a stone floor surface. If your retaining wall is 40 feet long by 2½ feet tall, the face is 100 square feet (40×2.5). If the wallstone you've selected covers 20 square feet per ton, you'll need 5.5 tons of wallstone (110/20=5.5) to build your wall and allow for 10 percent extra.

Boulder, Fieldstone, and Riprap. Ordering boulders for retaining walls, outcroppings, and other features is not as easy as the examples above. The best way to figure for large boulders, fieldstone of all sizes, and riprap is to explain to the salesperson the type of project, the range of boulder sizes you would like, and the dimensions of the project. The salesperson can then compute tonnage for you.

► Dress for hard work with gloves, heavy boots, and long sleeves when you go shopping for stone. You may have to pick through some big rocks to find the ones you want.

▲ Mesh cages hold stacks of riprap on pallets for handling with a forklift.

Sand, Gravel, and Base Materials. Sand, gravel, and other finer aggregates are measured by the cubic yard (cu.yd.) and sold by the ton. You need to calculate the volume, or how much space you need to fill, in cubic yards. This can then be easily converted to tons. Here's how to do it, using a flagstone pathway that is 3 feet wide and 35 feet long (including curves) as an example. You need to estimate the amount of crushed limestone for a 4-inch base and the amount of sand needed for a 1-inch layer on top of that. First compute the area of the pathway in square feet, multiplying length by width (3×35=105 sq. ft.). Then multiply the area by the multiplier shown for 4 inches in the table *opposite*. This gives you the volume of the path in cubic feet. (105×.33=34.65 cubic feet of material.) Round up to the next whole number, in this case 35. To convert cubic feet to cubic yards, divide cubic feet by 27 (one cubic yard equals 27 cubic feet). So 35 divided by 27 equals 1.29 yards. Round yards up to the nearest quarter yard; for this example, you'll need to order 1.5 yards.

To compute the sand, multiply the area by the multiplier corresponding to a 1-inch depth (105 times .083) to arrive at 9 cubic feet. Divide 9 by 27 to find you need ⅓ yard of sand.

Ask the salesperson to double-check your estimates before you order. (Your salesperson

▲ Cut stone is banded on pallets. Large pieces are too heavy to handle without equipment.

▲ Dead-blow hammers, hand sledges, masonry hammers, and brick sets are among the tools stone yards sell.

can also help you calculate the volume.) The salesperson will then convert the quantity in yards to tons, using different multipliers depending on the type of aggregate.

If you intend to haul the rock yourself and the stone yard has a vehicle scale, drive your vehicle, or vehicle and trailer, onto the scale to be weighed. Then drive to the stone you have selected. You can either load the stone yourself or pay a small loading fee to have it loaded. After loading, drive back to the scale for a second weighing. You'll receive a ticket noting the weight of your stone, which you take to the cashier. If it's a smaller yard without a scale, the salesperson will estimate the weight.

It is usually better to arrange for delivery of stone and pay a delivery fee, especially if you need large quanities for your project. A standard pickup truck might hold the volume of material you need, but may not be able to carry the weight.

SQUARE FOOTAGE TO CUBIC FEET CONVERSION TABLE

Depth in Inches	Multiplier
1	0.083
2	0.17
3	0.25
4	0.33
5	0.42
6	0.50
7	0.58
8	0.67
9	0.75
10	0.83
11	0.92
12	1.0

WORKING WITH STONE

Moving stone into the project area, positioning it, and altering its size can be hard work. Pace yourself, and rest when you get tired. Make safety your first concern. Always wear leather gloves and work boots (preferably steel-toed boots) when handling stone. Put on safety glasses or goggles any time you or someone near you saws, chisels, or splits stone.

2×4

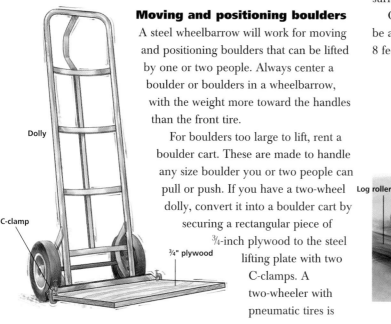

Boulder cart

best. You can probably move boulders in the 100- to 200-pound range this way; do not attempt to move any boulder that causes the lifting plate to bend.

You also can move a large boulder by placing it on a piece of ¾-inch plywood on top of log rollers. The rollers should be 6 inches in diameter or larger. Push the boulder on the rollers, moving each roller to the front as the back of the plywood clears it. This works well on paved surfaces, firm ground, or lawn.

Once boulders have been placed, they can be adjusted by lashing a 2×4 or stout pole about 8 feet long to the stone as shown *above*.

Moving and positioning boulders

A steel wheelbarrow will work for moving and positioning boulders that can be lifted by one or two people. Always center a boulder or boulders in a wheelbarrow, with the weight more toward the handles than the front tire.

For boulders too large to lift, rent a boulder cart. These are made to handle any size boulder you or two people can pull or push. If you have a two-wheel dolly, convert it into a boulder cart by securing a rectangular piece of ¾-inch plywood to the steel lifting plate with two C-clamps. A two-wheeler with pneumatic tires is

Dolly

C-clamp

¾" plywood

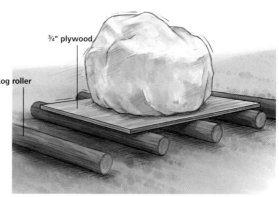

¾" plywood

Log roller

Breaking and shaping stone

A hydraulic jack splitter (*below*), if available for rental in your area, makes it easier to break wallstone and smaller pieces of flagstone. Center the stone in the breaking platform. Turn the handle on top to lower the jaw until it holds the stone firmly. Pump the foot pedal to raise the breaking platform until the stone breaks. Either straight or angled cuts are easy to make by placing the stone as shown. Always wear safety goggles when operating this type of machine.

If a hydraulic stone splitter is not available, you can cut all quarried stone (except fieldstone) with a 2- to 3-inch chisel and a hand sledge. Mark the break line with pencil, crayon, or marker. Place the chisel on the break line, and tap it firmly with the hand sledge until you've scored a line in the stone. (When breaking flagstone, score both the top and bottom surfaces.) Then place the stone so that the section to be removed hangs over the edge of another piece of flagstone or a 2×4 board. Strike the portion to be broken off firmly with the hand sledge or dead-blow hammer.

To break wallstone, score all four sides, then continue to deepen the score line while increasing the strength of the hand-sledge blows until the stone breaks. Wallstone often has small surface dimples or a jagged end that keeps the stone from stacking or butting closely. You can remove these bumps by cross-hatching the area. To do this, hold the stone between your knees. Using a 1-inch chisel and hand sledge, tap short parallel score lines across the area you want to remove. Then repeat with perpendicular score lines in a cross-hatch pattern. Bits of stone will start to splinter off immediately. Continue cross-hatching until the area is as smooth as you want. Always wear safety goggles for this work.

CROSS-HATCHING

STRAIGHT CUT WITH HYDRAULIC SPLITTER

Jaw

Breaking platform

Hydraulic jack

Foot pedal

ANGLE CUT WITH HYDRAULIC SPLITTER

CHAPTER HIGHLIGHTS

This chapter shows how to install flagstone, fieldstone, cobblestone, and other stone paths. It also includes instructions for walls, steps and staircases, and patios. You'll find information about stone slopes and rock gardens and directions for building water features with stone too.

PROJECTS IN STONE

Here's where the stone features shown in chapter 1 and the materials and techniques described in chapter 2 come together: This chapter shows how to actually build stone landscaping.

The ideas and design considerations for using stone in landscapes in the first chapter have probably whetted your appetite to add stone in your landscape. You have evaluated your yard usage, traffic patterns, and the style of your house. You have probably flagged photos of some stone features you want to duplicate or stone landscapes

with certain design elements you'd like to adapt to your yard. Chapter 2 showed you the tools and techniques employed for stonework, along with some fundamentals of laying out a landscape project and excavating the work area. And you learned how to select the appropriate stone material for your project, how to order the right amount from the stone yard, and how to handle the heavy stones.

All that's left now is the best part of the process: Constructing a unique stone feature on your property.

FLAGSTONE PATHS

Dry-Laid flagstone

Lay flagstone on top of a 1-inch layer of sand that has been spread over a compacted base layer. Use a bow rake with the tines turned up to level the sand; screeding is not necessary.

Remove at least half the flagstone from the pallet and spread it out where you can see the sizes and shapes of a dozen pieces. Begin laying pieces of flagstone (or flagstone steppers) along each edge of the path. Try to find and place pieces with a long side that follows the edge of the excavation. When necessary score and break a piece as shown *below*. As each piece is laid, set it into the sand by striking it with a large rubber hammer. Then step on all parts of the piece. If it's unstable, lift it out and add sand where needed to stabilize.

After the pathway edges have been set, fill in the gaps, scoring and breaking the stone as shown. Finish by sweeping sand or fine crushed gravel between all joints.

DRY-LAID FLAGSTONE

1 To fit flagstone tightly, place the next piece on top of the one to be broken, and mark the break line with pencil or chalk.

2 If a piece extends outside the pathway edge, draw the break line freehand to continue the edge.

3 Score the flagstone by placing a 2- to 4-inch chisel along the break line and tapping with a hand sledge. Score to a depth of ⅛ to ¼ inch. If you have a circular saw with a stone-cutting blade, cut a groove ¼ inch deep along the break line.

4 Place the flagstone on a piece of lumber as shown, and strike the waste end with a rubber or dead-blow hammer. If the flagstone flakes or breaks erratically, score the underside also. You'll soon get a feel for the amount of scoring your stone requires for clean breaks.

MORTARED FLAGSTONE

1 Trowel mortar onto the concrete base and smooth to 1 inch thick. Work in two or three stones at one time.

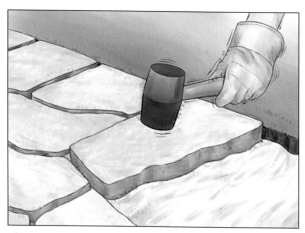

2 Set flagstone into the mortar by tapping the center of the stone with a large rubber hammer. After setting a few stones, remove the next few, and spread more mortar.

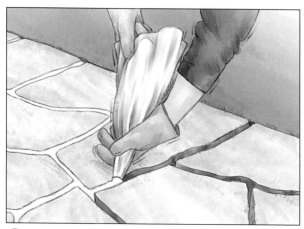

3 Let mortar set 24 hours, then grout joints, using the same type mortar mix. A thin trowel works, but a mortar bag makes filling narrow joints easier.

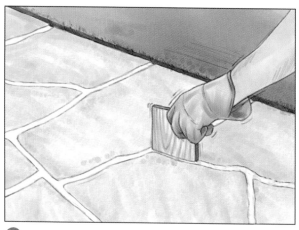

4 Smooth joints with the edge of a board or trowel. Keep a wet sponge handy to wipe mortar from stone surfaces before it sets.

Mortared flagstone

Refer to the base depth chart on *page 114*. If pouring the concrete base yourself, use a straight piece of lumber that fits just inside the width of the path to screed the concrete level. Brush the surface with a stiff broom to create a rough texture so the stone mortar will adhere. After the base concrete has cured for at least 72 hours, dry-lay your flagstone pieces on it. Do all cutting and fitting for the path. If the flagstone is porous, spray the stone with water a few hours before laying, so it doesn't absorb moisture from the mortar as it sets.

For setting stone make a mortar mix of one part sand, one part cement, and enough water to make a thick paste. Add water a little at a time. Remove two or three stones at one end, and proceed as shown *above*.

FIELDSTONE AND COBBLESTONE PATHS

Dry-laid

Lay cobblestones on compacted base material covered with 1 inch of sand (see chart, *page 114*). Fieldstones are different thicknesses, so excavate an inch or so deeper than your thickest stones. Lay a 1- to 2-inch base of sand, and install the largest stones first, spacing them throughout the length of the path. Then place the next largest stones, filling sand beneath them as necessary to keep the surface level. Continue filling with sand and placing stones, down to the smallest ones. If all your stones are relatively small, see Illustration 1 *below*.

Mortared

For mortared fieldstone pathways, trowel 2 inches of mortar over the compacted base and set the stones as shown in Illustrations 2 and 3.

SETTING STONES

1 To make a path with smaller stones, lightly till or break up the soil with a shovel. Place stones in soil, then set in place with a short length of 2×4 and a hammer.

2 For a mortared stone pathway, start with a 6-inch base layer of compacted gravel. Trowel in a 2-inch layer of stone mortar mix (see *page 127*) a few feet at a time. Press stones into the mortar.

3 Keep the surface level by pulling a straight board across the stones. When all stones are set, fill around them with mortar mix. Wipe excess mortar off stones with a damp sponge.

PATH PATTERNS

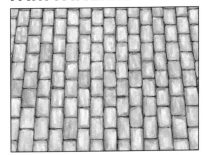

You can lay granite pavers and other stones of the same size and shape in a running pattern.

The square stones in this weave pattern are full stones that have been split and set on their split ends.

This basket-weave pattern invites a slower walking pace than the running pattern. It uses full stones.

Stepping-stones

A stepping-stone path is easy to install. Select flagstone steppers about the same size and shape. Steppers 2 inches thick or thicker will be the most stable. A compacted gravel base is not necessary, even in cold climates. Do not excavate the entire pathway; simply dig a recess for each stone as shown in the illustrations.

STEPPING-STONES

1 Lay the stones in place on the ground. Adjust the layout to create the curves and spacing you prefer.

2 Cut the sod or score the soil around each stepper with a heavy-bladed knife or wallboard saw.

3 Place the stone to the side, then dig out the area to the depth of the stone's thickness plus 1 inch.

4 Shovel a 1-inch layer of sand into the recess and smooth it.

5 Position the stone and set it by stomping or jumping on the center of the stone.

LAYOUTS FOR STEPPING-STONE PATHS

Flagstone steppers are often placed single file, as shown at right in the illustration. If you'd like to broaden the path, choose steppers with an oblong shape, and stagger them as shown at the left of the illustration.

OTHER PATHS

Plastic paver edging on top of the compacted gravel base (see *page 115*) prevents the stones along the edge from shifting out of the grid over time.

Dry-laid cut stone

Set the edging then use it as a guide for screeding the 1-inch layer of sand, as shown in the illustrations *below*. Set the bottom screed board so that the finished depth of screeded sand brings the surface of the cut stone ½ inch above the plastic edge. After screeding, tamp the sand firmly with a hand tamper. Fill in any low spots and tamp, add a little sand, then screed again.

The thickness of cut stone can vary so much that many landscapers do not screed the sand layer. They simply rake the sand smooth, then set the stone, adding and tamping sand before setting thinner pieces. You don't need to screed if the thickness of your cut stone varies more than ⅜ inch.

Mortared cut stone

Dry-lay cut stone directly on the poured concrete slab to check for fit, and determine if any pieces need to be cut. Spacing is up to you, but it should be uniform, between ¼ and ½ inch. Mark stone to be cut with a felt-tip marker and cut with a circular saw that has a diamond-tipped masonry blade. Remove the stone and place it alongside the path where it will be laid.

Prepare the base and install the stone as you would mortared flagstone (see *page 127*), except you will need to screed the stone mortar. Screed as large an area as you can finish in 15 minutes.

DRY-LAID CUT STONE

1 Screed sand by pulling the screed board along the top of the plastic edging. Screed to a depth that puts the stone surface ½ inch above the edging.

2 Whether dry-laid or mortared, set each stone by tapping with a rubber hammer. Space the stones at least ¼ inch apart to allow for slight variances in the dimensions of the stone.

GRAVEL

① Edge gravel paths with steel or plastic edging, brick, or cobblestone. Dump finish gravel onto a compacted base and distribute into smaller piles with a long-handled round-nose shovel.

② Spread the gravel with a bow rake, then turn the rake tines up to smooth the surface. Wet the gravel to clean and help settle it. Finish by tamping the path with a hand tamper or rolling it with a lawn roller.

③ Gravel pathways allow for great flexibility in design.

Gravel

After preparing the base (see *pages 114–115*), follow the steps *above*.

Mixed materials and mosaics

For pathways of mixed materials, prepare the base as you would for flagstone (see *pages 114–115*). Examine the thickness of the materials ahead of time; you may find great variances in the thickness of the stones. If so, excavate deep enough to put in a 2- to 3-inch sand layer.

Install dry-laid mosaic paths the same way as fieldstone pathways. Mortared mosaic paths are installed the same way as mortared fieldstone pathways. Both are described on *page 128*.

MIXED MATERIALS

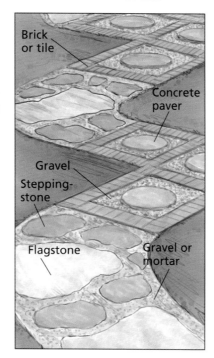

Brick or tile
Concrete paver
Gravel
Stepping-stone
Flagstone
Gravel or mortar

Cut stone
Cut stone or paver
Decorative stone or fieldstone
Gravel

RETAINING WALLS

Before starting, make sure that the wall you want to build is a practical do-it-yourself project. The size of boulders used in construction depends on the height of the wall; boulder retaining walls more than 4 feet tall require stacking boulders that are heavier than two strong adults can lift. (For more information, see *pages 38–41*.) Walls of this size should be professionally built.

Start the wall by excavating 6 inches deep for the first course (layer) of boulders. Unless the ground is swampy or otherwise unstable, you do not need a layer of compacted base material in the excavation. Cut a piece of 4-foot-wide, heavy-duty landscape fabric the same length as the wall. Place the long edge of the fabric across the first course excavation and

secure it with long nails or spikes. Drape the remainder of the fabric, the portion that will be between the boulders and the fill material, on the excavated slope behind the wall. Hold the fabric in place with spikes.

Use the largest, heaviest boulders for the first course. Transport and position boulders as shown on *page 122*. Select boulders that fit tightly side-by-side. (Some gaps are inevitable.) After setting the first course, lay the landscape fabric over the front of the boulders and fill in the area behind the boulders with a gravel-soil mix. Compact it by stomping it firmly with your feet or with a tamper. Drape the landscape fabric back against the slope.

Place the boulders for the second and subsequent courses, fitting them together as

BOULDER WALL

A boulder retaining wall that looks like stacked cannonballs, *right*, isn't as natural appearing as a wall built with a greater variety of stone sizes and shapes, *below right*. If you select the boulders yourself at the stone yard, get some that are oblong, pear-shaped, and other shapes.

If the boulders will be delivered, be sure the load includes boulders of different shapes and sizes to help fill gaps. You'll develop a talent for eyeing and placing boulders of different sizes that fit snugly and match the contours of the boulders below them.

tightly as possible. For safety, set each course back slightly so the wall angles backward 1 foot for every 3 feet of height. After laying each course, pull the landscape fabric over the front of each course, then backfill with a gravel-soil mix, tamping it firmly.

WALLSTONE RETAINING WALL

1 For wallstone retaining walls, excavate and install a 4-inch compacted base layer, then 1 inch of sand. Install the first course with at least 1 inch below ground level.

2 Continue with each course, selecting or breaking stone so that stones in each course overlap the end gaps of the previous course, as in a brick wall.

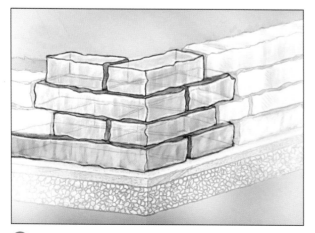

3 If your wall has a corner, stack stones so they interlock. You'll probably have to break stones to fit.

4 Save some thinner wallstones to use as the capstones, or a top course, as shown.

FREESTANDING WALLS

The base width of the wall should be at least two-thirds of the wall height. (Multiply the wall height by .67 to determine the base width.)

Mortared wall

Mortared walls are constructed on a poured concrete footing incorporating reinforcement bar or steel mesh. Unless you have done this type of concrete work before, consider hiring a professional contractor to excavate and pour the footing, especially in northern regions where the slab must extend below the frost line. The concrete footing should be 8 inches wider than the base width so the concrete extends 4 inches on each side.

Dry-stack wall

Build a dry-stack wall on a compacted gravel base (see base chart on *page 114*). Make the gravel base 4 inches wider than the base width of the wall, so it extends 2 inches past the face of the wall along each side. Bluestone, cut

MORTARED WALL

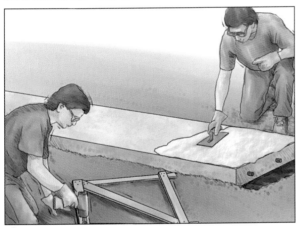

1 Build batter frames for each end of the wall. Allow 2 inches of batter (inward slope) for every 2 feet of height. Trowel a 1-inch layer of stone mortar (see "mortar" in the Glossary) along the first 2 feet of slab.

2 Set a bondstone—a stone that extends the width of the wall—across the end, then set stone on both sides of the wall, mortaring all joints as you go. Pack the center area with stone, rubble, and mortar. Scrape all joints with the trowel tip before the mortar sets, and clean stones with a damp sponge as you work.

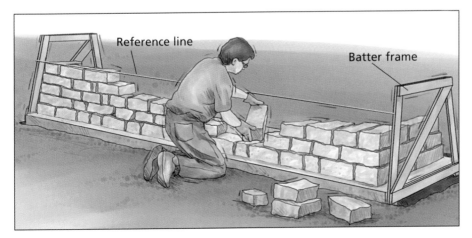

Reference line

Batter frame

3 Place batter frames at each end and stretch strings to maintain the slope. You can also use a batter gauge (see *page 103*). Apply fresh mortar to the top of stones already in place as you build each course. Work courses from each end to the middle. Place bondstones that span the wall width for every 10 square feet of wall surface area. Finish with capstones that span the wall.

wallstone, fieldstone, and flagstone are all good materials for a dry-stack wall. Break flagstone into smaller pieces by dropping large pieces on top of a fieldstone. If you construct a fieldstone wall, use stones of about the same size. Finding long fieldstones for bond stones or capstones will be difficult; instead carefully fit the stones snugly, and maintain proper batter (inward slope), even on shorter walls.

DRY-STACK WALL

1 Place a bondstone at one end, then continue to place stones along each side of the wall. Work courses from each end so they meet in the middle.

2 Pack the center gap tightly with stone and rubble. Bondstones that span the entire width of the wall are important. Place one bondstone for every 6 square feet of wall surface area.

3 Fill gaps with smaller pieces and tap them in with a dead-blow hammer. Maintain proper batter as you build the wall, as shown on the *opposite page*.

4 Finish with capstones that span the wall. The wall will last longer if you mortar the middle two-thirds of the capstones (so the mortar holds but is not seen).

5 Consider constructing a low farmer's wall out of mixed stone materials. These can be mortared or dry-stacked.

STEPS AND STAIRCASES

Before installing steps and staircases, determine how many steps are needed for the slope. First calculate the height of the slope, called the *rise*. Next calculate the run–the length of the slope, which is the distance between the first step and the last. Determine the rise and run of the slope with a straight board, a level, and a tape measure, as shown *below*.

step on; the riser is the vertical face between treads, as shown in the illustration at *below*. It's important to keep the depth of the tread and height of the riser in a pleasing proportion so the steps look graceful and are safe.

You can do that by relying on tread and riser dimensions that have been established over time. The general rule is that the depth of the tread plus twice the height of the riser should equal 25 to 27 inches. So a spacious 17-inch tread looks best with a relatively low 5-inch riser ($5\times2+17=27$). A 7-inch riser would make the 17-inch step look too tall but would look right for a tread 12 inches deep ($7\times2+12=26$). Make stair treads 11 inches or more deep for safety.

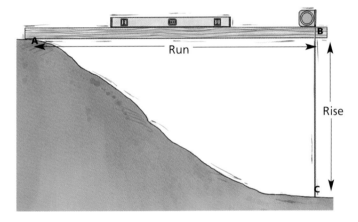

Extend a straight 2×4 or other board from the top of the slope so that the end extends over the bottom of the slope. While someone holds the 2×4 level, measure the run from A to B (illustration *above*). Then measure the rise from B to C. Record both measurements in inches.

Next, decide how tall and deep the steps will be. The tread is the horizontal surface that you

Here are the most common tread-to-riser measurements for stone steps in the landscape:

Riser	Tread
5 in.	15–17 in.
5½ in.	14–16 in.
6 in.	13–15 in.
6½ in.	12–14 in.
7 in.	11–13 in.
8 in.	11 in.

To compute the number of steps needed for your slope, divide the rise (in inches) by the height of the riser you want. If the rise is 68 inches and you want 5-inch risers, divide

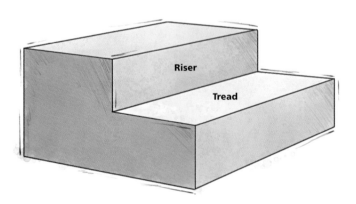

68 inches by 5 inches. The result is 13.6. When the result is a number with a fraction, drop the fraction. So in this example, you will need 13 steps to climb the slope. Next make sure the tread depth that's appropriate for your riser height will cover the run.

A 5-inch riser calls for a tread depth of 15 to 17 inches. If your run is 208 inches, divide that distance by the number of steps to determine the tread depth for each step. The resulting tread depth of 16 inches (208 inches/13=16 inches) falls within the recommended size range.

You also can multiply the number of steps by the minimum tread depth (13×15 inches=195 inches) and maximum tread depth (13×17 inches=221 inches) to determine a range of run lengths that would work with 5-inch risers. Remember you can grade the slope, or create a landing or two to help the steps fit.

DESIGNING STEPS

Curve a stone staircase whenever possible. This is relatively easy to do on a gradual slope.

Quarried steps come in a variety of sizes. Calculate the thickness (riser) so the step overlaps the stone below enough for stability and proper tread proportion.

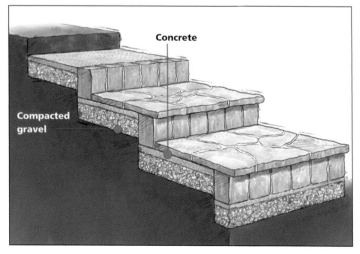

Concrete

Compacted gravel

To install mortared steps, excavate each step and install base material as you would for a mortared cut-stone patio (see base depth chart on *page 114*).

DRY-LAID FLAGSTONE PATIOS

Spread the flagstone around the project area so you can see all the sizes and shapes. Select a large piece and place it at the foot of the patio door. If you know where a dining set or barbecue grill will be, place larger pieces there.

How often you have to break flagstone to fit neatly is up to you. If you are content with a looser, more country look, you can lay a flagstone patio without chiseling a single piece. Select and place pieces around the edge that best match the contour. Work to the center, placing large pieces throughout the area and fitting them as best you can. Maintain 1- to 2-inch spacing. As you set each piece, take a little jump step and land with both feet squarely in the center to set it firmly in the sand. Step to each edge. If the piece rocks at all, lift the piece out and add or remove sand to stabilize it. The impression left by the slab (or lack of impression) will usually show you spots where you need to add or remove sand.

Next work with smaller pieces to fill gaps. Have a small fieldstone nearby. When you can no longer fit pieces, take a few of the largest unused pieces and drop them squarely on the fieldstone. The flagstone slabs will break into smaller pieces. Use these and continue to break pieces until you have filled all gaps. Watch for triangle-shaped pieces; they always work well to fill gaps.

To lay a more tightly fitted patio, score and break pieces to fit between larger stones (see *page 126*). Space stones ½ to 1 inch apart. Maintaining spacing less than ½ inch is hard work and takes a long time.

Finish by sweeping sand, pea gravel, or finely crushed granite across the patio. If you want moss or grass between the stones, dig out the sand and compacted gravel around each flagstone to 4 inches deep, using a thin flat stick. Fill the spaces with garden soil, and tamp.

DRY-LAID PATIO

1 Lay edge pieces first. Use the largest pieces at entrances, under furniture, and for grilling areas.

2 Space large pieces throughout the patio to fill in the middle. Place stones like bricks to prevent continuous straight channels across the surface.

MORTARED FLAGSTONE PATIOS

Build the base. (See the chart on *page 114*.) Spread out the flagstones and dry-lay all pieces on the concrete slab, as described on the *opposite page*. If the flagstone is porous, wet it thoroughly for a few hours before laying it. Score and break stones as necessary to maintain uniform ¹⁄₂- to 1-inch spacing. Follow the steps *below* for mortaring the patio. Work from one side to the other so you do not step on freshly mortared pieces.

MORTARED PATIO

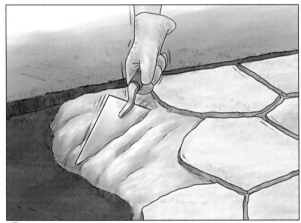

1 Remove two or three stones at an edge. Trowel mortar onto the concrete slab and smooth it to 1 inch thick.

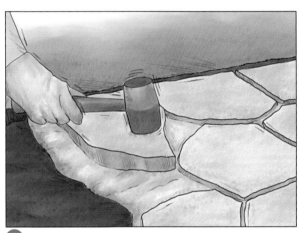

2 Set flagstone into mortar by tapping each piece firmly in the center with a large rubber hammer. After setting a few stones, remove the next few, and spread more mortar.

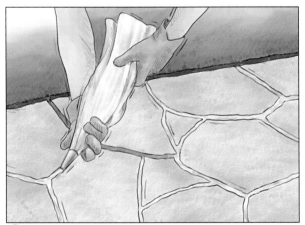

3 Let mortar set 24 hours, then grout joints with stone mortar mix. You can do this using a narrow trowel, but a mortar bag, *above*, is better, especially for narrow joints.

4 Smooth joints with a trowel tip or a stick. Keep a wet sponge handy to wipe mortar from the surface before it sets.

Cut-Stone Patios

nstall plastic paver edging along one side of the patio on top of the compacted gravel base (see *pages 114–115*). If the patio extends from the house, set the edging on one of the sides of the patio that is perpendicular to the house. Edging for the remaining sides will be installed after all stones have been laid, so the edging will fit tightly against the stone.

Verify that the perimeter dimensions of your patio accommodate the sizes of your stone. It's simplest to design a patio with dimensions in 6- or 12-inch increments. If your stone sizes (in inches) are 12×12, 12×18, 12×24, 18×18, and 18×24, a patio that measures 15 feet by 24 feet, 6 inches will require less stone breaking than one that measures, for example, 15 feet, 4 inches by 24 feet, 8 inches. Excavate and install base material in an area slightly larger than the finished patio. Allow an extra 6 inches of compacted gravel on all sides, except a side

butting up to a house or other structure.

Spread 1 inch of sand evenly over the compacted gravel base, using a bow rake with the tines facing up. Rough-screed the sand until it appears uniformly level. Screed with a straight board 3 feet long, held in one hand. Pull the sand from high spots to low ones in broad, curving strokes. You don't need to screed the sand layer perfectly for cut stone and you don't need to tamp. Screeding large areas perfectly level is time consuming and difficult. Plus there is usually so much variance in the thickness of cut stone that screeding and tamping the sand base makes thicker pieces of stone stick up too high in the finished patio.

Establish a pattern and repeat it when working with cut stone. You should use three to five different sizes of stone. Experiment with stone placement on a stretch of lawn. Lay out a combination that uses one of the largest pieces

CUT-STONE PATIO

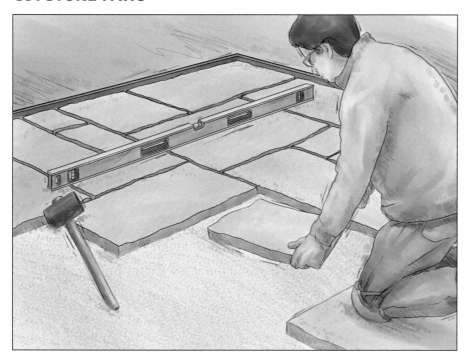

1 Work from a stone that has already been laid. Check often with a 4-foot level to ensure that the patio is level.

and three or four others of varying size. They should form a large square or rectangle. Even if they do not, design a pattern for placement of the pieces that you can repeat across the patio. If the patio is adjacent to the house, establish your stone pattern so that a large piece is laid at the foot of the patio door. Laying cut stone in a pattern ensures that pieces of all sizes will be spread evenly across the patio.

If the patio extends from the home's exterior wall, set the first stone in the corner of the exterior wall and the plastic edging. Work from outside the patio area. (Have a few 2×3-foot sheets of ½-inch plywood handy to place on the sand as work platforms when two people are setting larger stones.)

Check each stone for level, using a 12-inch level. Set the stone with a rubber hammer. Pound hard to set the stone, then tap to level it. Continue to lay and set stone along the side extending from the corner, then work evenly across the patio. Check each stone for level. Also frequently check across several stones with a 4-foot level to ensure that the patio is level. You can stand on the stones you have already set to lay others.

As you approach the edges of your patio, you may be able to alter your pattern slightly so that you can finish with a straight edge. If not, mark and cut stones using a circular saw with a diamond-tipped stone blade.

Remove any sand outside the perimeter edge of the stone without removing any from under the stone. Slide the remaining plastic edging pieces on top of the compacted gravel base until they are tight against the stone edge. Set with spikes (see *page 115*).

2 To make a curved edge on a cut-stone patio, set stones so they extend outside of the curve. Mark the curve with chalk or a pencil, then cut along the line with a circular saw and a stone blade.

SEATING AND CONTAINER SPACES

▼ Widen a pathway to create a rest stop. Here the area is slightly longer than the bench to make room for a single plant container.

Any type of stone surface makes a good seating space or a place to put potted plants or decorative planters. Excavate, prepare base material, and install the stone surface as you would a pathway or patio. See layout and excavation techniques on *pages 104–113*. Build an appropriate base, as shown on the chart on *page 114*. Then install the paving, following instructions for flagstone (*pages 126–127*), fieldstone and cobblestone (*page 128*), cut stone (*page 130*), or gravel, mixed materials, and mosaic (*page 131*).

Stone edging

Stone edging best defines flower, tree, and shrub beds. It also makes an excellent edging for raised beds. Excavate to 3 inches deep along the edge of the bed and loosen the soil that remains. Base material is not necessary for edging. Place the stone in the excavation so that it fits snugly. If you build a raised bed, first lay the stone, then place a 1- or 2-foot-wide strip of landscape fabric against the back of the stone before backfilling, as shown *below*.

EDGING

1 Select fieldstones that are about the same height, but with slightly different shapes, spacing the wider stones one or two stones apart.

2 Small granite traprock (riprap) makes a tight edging that requires careful fitting of each stone.

3 To raise a bed more than 12 inches, install one- and two-course edging, all of the same type of stone or of mixed materials.

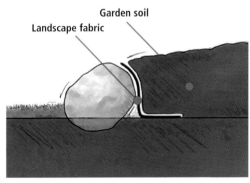

Garden soil
Landscape fabric

ROCK SLOPES

F irst decide on the purpose of your slope. You can either create a rock (alpine) garden and grow plants amidst the stone or have the stone itself be the feature, with little or no emphasis on plants. Follow the steps *below* for a boulder slope.

If you want to plant small shrubs and perennials in a rock garden, build your rock slope where it will have full sun. Excavate 20 inches deep, then fill with 4 inches of gravel and sand. Then add 14 inches of garden soil, instead of filling with gravel and sand as described

below. Step the soil in so it is firm, but not compacted. Place the boulders as shown in Step 2. You need to create fairly level spaces between the boulders for growing plants. Let stone cover less of the area for a rock garden—40 to 60 percent. Water the entire area well so the boulders settle. Allow the soil to dry before planting.

Plant the spaces between the boulders. (See chapter 4 for more information on plants.) Plant at least 10 inches away from boulders, and be sure to allow enough room for the mature sizes

BOULDER SLOPE

1 Choose an area on a gentle slope. If the soil drains well, excavate to 6 inches deep. If drainage is a concern, excavate to 20 inches deep and fill with a 14-inch base of one part clean gravel and one part sand. Compacting is not necessary.

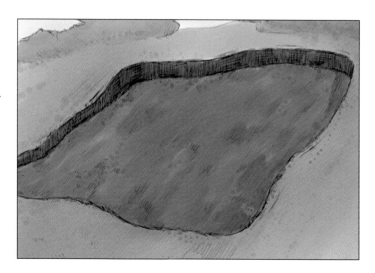

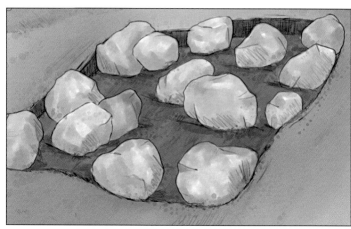

2 Place boulders in natural-looking combinations: a single boulder, two bumping together, and two together with a third, smaller stone off to one side. Stone should cover 50 to 70 percent of the area.

BOULDER SLOPE (continued from page 143)

of perennials, annuals, and dwarf conifers. After planting, mulch with small (⅛- to ½-inch) gravel, pea gravel, or small river stone. A rock garden in full sun will need ample water, some plants as often as every other day in the hottest and sunniest parts of summer.

3 Finish by installing a 4-inch layer of one part clean gravel and one part sand, followed by a 2-inch top layer of clean gravel or river stone.

A SLAB GARDEN

A slab garden is an area that is nearly all stone, carefully set so that the lines of the stone are parallel, resembling one large outcropping that has split over time.

You may find split rock for slabs at the stone yard. If not, ask if split slabs are available by special order.

Excavate for a slab garden as you would a rock slope (see *page 143*), then lay out the slabs in the prepared area. Leave gaps between the stones of a few inches to a foot. Pack around the base of the slab with gravel or a mixture of one part gravel and one part sand. Fill the remainder with gardening soil if you want to grow plants in the gaps between the slabs.

OUTCROPPINGS AND ACCENTS

Place boulders for outcroppings and accents so they appear natural. Look at other landscapes with outcroppings and see what you do and don't like about the way the boulders are placed. Study photos of outcroppings and boulders in natural landscapes to get other ideas.

Excavate 6 inches deep in the area where one or more boulders will be placed. Dig deeper if a large portion of a boulder will be buried to make a more attractive feature. Base material isn't needed in the hole unless the ground is swampy or otherwise unstable.

The most common mistake in creating an outcropping is using boulders that are too small. Part of the boulder will be hidden underground, and a few inches of mulch on the ground can hide most of a boulder that looked quite large when sitting on the surface.

Boulder sizes vary in natural settings, so use stones of different sizes to make your feature look realistic. Groupings of odd numbers look best. An outcropping of two stones is fine as long as there's a third stone or another outcropping nearby, as shown *above right*.

A long, narrow outcropping like the one at *right* makes a rustic, informal wall that can define an outdoor room or ring a patio. Use boulders in a variety of sizes. Place small stones randomly around the boulder bases to soften the outcropping.

CUT-STONE PLANTING BOXES AND CONTAINERS

Building planter boxes is similar to installing stone walls. Follow the layout and excavation techniques on *pages 104–113*. Construction techniques for walls are on *pages 134–135*.

A stone planting box or container will probably require construction of more corners than a typical wall; page 133 shows the method for building corners with wallstone. Before you fill the planter with garden soil, line the inside of the box with landscape fabric to prevent soil erosion through small gaps in the stone.

You do not need to slope walls inward for stone container boxes and planters that are 3 feet tall or less.

PLANTING BOX

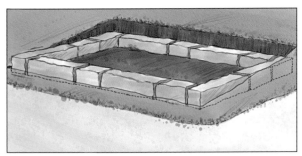

1 If the ground slopes, dig a flat and level excavation. Place a long level on the ground in the direction of the slope and check for level. Install base material and check for level again after the base material has been compacted. Lay a full course of stone for the first one, even if that course (or more) will be underground. Check for level on all sides of the box as stones are placed.

3 Lay capstones to finish. Break stones for the corners at a 45-degree angle, either by scoring and breaking with a chisel and hand sledge or with a hydraulic stone splitter (see *page 103*). Capstones may be mortared, but if the rest of the wall is dry-laid, use mortar sparingly so it does not show on the outside of the box.

PLANTER IDEAS

2 Container boxes are an attractive focal point when built out from the house as a three-sided box. Staple thick plastic or rubber liner on the wall of the house that will have soil packed against it. Trim the liner so it doesn't show.

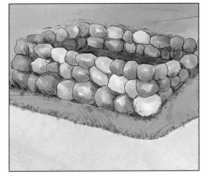

4 Dry-stacked stone planter boxes lend a rustic, old-world feel to the landscape. Some stone supply yards sell irregular flagstone cut into 8- to 10-inch strips, just right for a box.

PEBBLE AND BOULDER FOUNTAINS

Determine the size of the fountain, which will be the diameter of the hole you dig to hold water. The smallest practical size is 18 inches in diameter. The hole for a large pebble fountain can be 3 or 4 feet in diameter. For any size, dig a hole 16 inches deep with nearly vertical sides.

Line the hole with rubber pond liner, as shown in the illustration. If you use a rigid plastic pond liner, dig the hole to fit the liner. Be sure to buy a liner that is at least 16 inches deep.

Buy a pump, a fountainhead, and a riser pipe to connect the fountainhead to the pump. The landscape supply dealer can help you select the right size pump. The riser pipe should be long enough to extend at least 4 inches above grade. (Some can be adjusted over a range of a few inches.) Fountainheads come in several spray styles: Some bubble water like a drinking fountain, some spray it straight up, and some fan the water into an umbrella shape. Some fountainheads are adjustable. Be sure the pump's electrical cord is long enough to run along the bottom of the pond and up the side to the electrical outlet, which must be on dry land beyond the perimeter of the fountain.

Attach the riser pipe and fountainhead to the pump. Place the pump on a brick in the bottom of the pond (see illustration) so it will not sit in sediment that could clog it. The pump should have an intake filter. Plug the pump into a GFCI (ground fault circuit interrupter) outlet for safety. If there is no existing outlet and you want to install one yourself, consult a wiring manual and check local building codes. Run the electrical line from the house to the GFCI outlet through plastic conduit buried 16 inches deep to protect it from being sliced by a shovel. You can have the wiring and outlet installed by an electrician.

Lay rigid metal grid, available from hardware and landscape supply stores, across

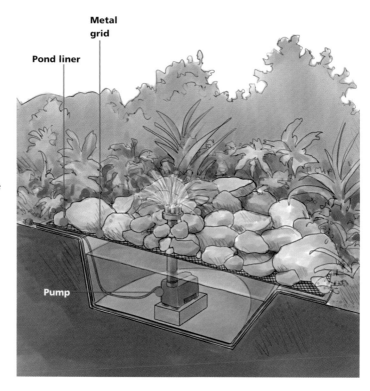

Metal grid

Pond liner

Pump

the pond. Cut the grid with tin snips to the shape of the pond, making it large enough to extend 6 inches beyond the perimeter. Cut a 6-inch-square hole directly over the pump so you can reach the pump through the grid. In a large pond, stack bricks or cement blocks near the pump to support the steel grid.

Fill the pond with water until it is about 1 inch from overflowing. Arrange stones of different shapes, colors, and sizes in layers on the grid. Do not put too much weight on the grid. Adjust the riser height—cut it, if necessary— to place the fountainhead just below the height of the stones. Plug in the pump, and move the stones for the best effect.

Instructions for building a boulder fountain are on the *next page*.

PEBBLE AND BOULDER FOUNTAINS (CONTINUED)

Boulder fountain

Boulders that have one or more holes drilled through them for use as boulder fountains are available at some landscape supply yards as well as pond and fountain retailers. Construct the fountain the same way as a pebble fountain, described on the *previous page*, except stack bricks or blocks beside the pump to support the weight of the boulder, as shown at *right*. Instead of a rigid riser pipe, use flexible plastic tubing to connect the fountainhead to the pump. Buy tubing that fits through the hole in the boulder.

CREATING A RUIN

Most ruins take the form of a portion of wall that appears very old. The wall section can be mortared or dry-stacked, and is built so it appears to have partially crumbled over time. Lay some stones on the ground to represent those that have fallen away. Some of them would be partially buried. You also could include a section of stone floor. A partial window opening or a window frame adds authenticity. Follow layout and excavation techniques on *pages 106–113*. For information about building walls, see *pages 134–135*. A low ruin, even mortared, could be built without concrete footings.

POOLS, PONDS, AND WATERFALLS

Pools and waterfalls usually need a deep excavation, so first call your local utilities and have them mark underground utility lines (see *page 104*). This section describes construction of pools and waterfalls using flexible rubber pond liners. Rigid preformed plastic ponds and waterfall units are also available, but the flexible rubber pond liners are easier to install, offer more design options, and help create a more natural-looking water garden than the rigid plastic ponds and waterfall kits. People often remove a rigid preformed unit just a few years after installation and replace it with a water feature that has a flexible rubber pond liner.

Install the rubber liner with both a 1-inch layer of sand and underlayment, a nonwoven fabric such as Geotextile Underlay, under it. Many pond plans and instructions recommend one or the other, but using both helps prevent puncturing the liner during construction. Many professional landscapers lay both the sand layer and underlayment.

POND

① Remove sod or the top layer of plant growth across the entire pond area. During excavation, fully remove tree and shrub roots. Dig a rim 3 inches deep and 12 inches wide outside the actual pond outline. The edge of the pond liner will lie in this rim, held in place by stone.

② Make the ledge 12 inches wide and between 3 and 6 inches below grade. This ledge will support the stone and plants that naturalize the edge. This first ledge doesn't need to go all the way around the pond. You can make one area taper gradually deeper, like a gravel beach into a lake. Check to be sure your excavation is level in all directions, especially around the top edge.

③ Make another ledge at least 10 inches below the first, 12 to 18 inches wide. Next excavate the center section so that the pond is at least 24 inches deep. In regions where winter temperatures drop below −20 degrees Fahrenheit, dig the pond 40 inches deep if you want to keep the pond from freezing solid so fish can overwinter. (You can use a stock-tank heater in a shallower pond to keep fish through the winter too.)

POND (continued from page 149)

④ Spread 1 inch of sand on all horizontal surfaces in the pool. This protects the liner from sharp rocks in the excavation and cushions it to protect it from the weight of larger stones placed on top of the liner.

⑤ Install underlayment over the sand layer. This fabric adds another layer of protection to prevent liner punctures. You can walk on the underlayment to conform it to the shape of the pond. Next install a high-quality EPDM rubber pond liner on top of the underlayment. Step carefully on the rubber liner as you move it around to conform to the excavation.

ENSURING WATER QUALITY

Maintaining good water quality is essential for any size pond. The health of plants and fish in your pond revolves around the nitrogen cycle. The pond creates nitrogen, in the form of ammonia, from fish waste, uneaten fish food, and plant debris. Natural enzymes and nitrifying bacteria consume the ammonia and turn it into nitrite, which oxidizes into nitrate. Nitrate doesn't harm water quality and is beneficial to plants.

When this system is out of balance, ammonia builds up faster than it can be turned into nitrate, the pond develops excess algae, and fish and plant health suffers. To protect against this, circulate and filter water. Mechanical filters, biological filters, and filters that combine both principles are available. Ask your pond supply retailer to help you choose the best system for your water feature.

6 Fill the pond with water before trimming the rubber liner to final size or placing any stone. The liner must be free to shift slightly while the weight of the water pushes it into the contours of the pond. After the pond is full, trim away excess liner 12 inches from the edge of the pool. Place rocks and stones around the perimeter.

FIGURING WATER VOLUME OF A POOL

For figuring pump sizes, and to help when treating water with chemicals, you need to know how many gallons of water your pond holds. Here's how to do that:

Calculate all dimensions in feet. First calculate the surface area of the pond, as shown. Multiply the surface area by the average depth of the pond to find volume. Multiply volume by 7.48 to find capacity in gallons.

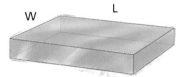

SURFACE AREA OF RECTANGULAR OR SQUARE POND: Multiply width by length to find surface area.

SURFACE AREA OF A CIRCULAR POND: Measure the length from center to edge (radius). Multiply that figure by itself, and then by 3.14 to find surface area.

SURFACE AREA OF AN OBLONG POND: Divide the pond into a square (or rectangle) and two half circles. Calculate the area of the square, then consider the two half circles as one full circle and calculate its surface area.

SURFACE AREA OF OVAL POND: Measure from the center to the farthest edge, then from the center to the nearest edge. Multiply the first figure by the second, and the result by 3.14 to find surface area.

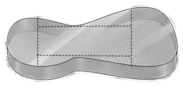

SURFACE AREA OF AN IRREGULAR POND: Divide the pond into simple units (*above*, a rectangle, triangles, and semicircles) and figure the area of each.

POND (continued from page 151)

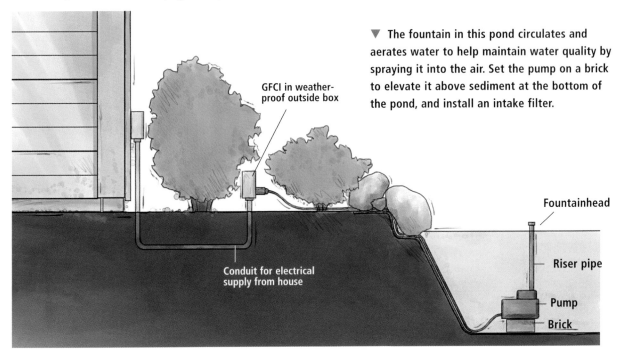

▼ The fountain in this pond circulates and aerates water to help maintain water quality by spraying it into the air. Set the pump on a brick to elevate it above sediment at the bottom of the pond, and install an intake filter.

GFCI in weather-proof outside box

Conduit for electrical supply from house

Fountainhead

Riser pipe

Pump

Brick

A pump helps maintain better water quality in a garden pond. If you will have fish in your pond, you must have a pump. The pump can supply a fountain, as shown above, or circulate water through a filtration and aeration system, which can be out of sight. If the pond only holds plants, you do not need a pump.

Set the pump on a brick at the deepest point in the pond to keep it above the sediment that can settle to the bottom of the pond. The pump must be plugged into a GFCI (ground fault circuit interrupter) receptacle. If there is not one near the pond, install one or have one installed by an electrician (see *page 147*).

▼ This cross section shows additional excavation options for plants. Ledges do not need to be the same depth. The upper ledge can taper so stones at the edge are partially submerged. Elevate plant containers to proper depth by placing them on stacked bricks or a cement block.

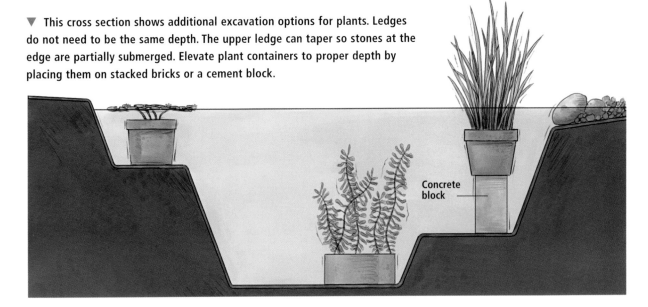

Concrete block

POND WITH WATERFALLS

▲ A stream with a series of waterfalls ending in a pond follows the same principles as building a pond. Excavate the streambed at least 8 inches deep. Place 1 inch of sand and underlayment in both the stream and the pond. Install the rubber liner in two pieces, one for the stream and the other for the pond. Lap the end of the stream liner over the edge of the pond liner, and seal the joint with marine silicone.

CHOOSING PUMPS

The number to consider when selecting a pump is the flow rate, measured in gallons per hour (gph). Your pond supply retailer will be able to recommend the best pump for your water feature if you know this information:

■ **Pond:** Amount of water in your pond in gallons (see *page 151*), fountain type, and filter type.

■ **Stream:** Number of gallons in holding pond, distance from pump to start of the stream, height of discharge point (start of stream) above pump (known as head or lift), and width and depth of water in stream.

■ **Waterfall:** Number of gallons in holding pond, distance from pump to the start of the waterfall, height of discharge point above pump (top of waterfall), and preferred width of water over waterfall.

If you have a choice, use the larger pump. You can reduce its flow with a valve in the outflow line, but you can't increase the flow of a pump that's too small.

POND WITH WATERFALLS (continued from page 153)

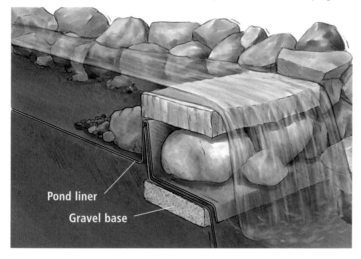

Pond liner

Gravel base

Building a single-step waterfall

In a waterfall system, the pond becomes the holding area for water flowing over the fall. An upper, smaller pond serves as the waterfall reservoir. A pump in the lower pond pumps water into the upper reservoir through plastic pipe. Then gravity takes over.

First excavate the lower pond (see *page 149*), then excavate the reservoir. The upper reservoir's size is optional, but it should hold at least 5 gallons of water and have a minimum depth of 8 inches (24 inches if it will contain fish). The water surface of the reservoir (where it starts to fall) should be at least 12 inches above the water surface in the lower pond.

The greater this distance, the greater the sound and visual attraction of the waterfall.

Excavate a ledge between the two ponds to hold one or more stones that will support the main waterfall lip stone. The top surface of the lip stone must be at the surface of the water in the reservoir. Determine the ledge location based on the thickness of the lip stone and the thickness of the supporting stones, then excavate a few inches deeper to allow for a 2-inch layer of sand or crushed gravel on the ledge. This will prevent the support stones from settling deeper than intended.

Install a sand layer, underlayment, and rubber liner in the bottom pond (see *page 150*). Extend the liner over the pond floor and up over the top face of the ledge (see illustration, *above left*). Install sand, underlayment, and liner for the upper reservoir. Lap the reservoir liner over the lower pond liner so it ends a few inches below the bottom of the ledge, as shown. Bond the two liners with marine silicone.

Fill the lower pond with water, then place the support stones and lip stone. Install the pump in the lower pond, and run a flexible plastic water line from the pump discharge fitting up the edge of the waterfall to the reservoir. Place stones around the edge of the pond, and the edges of the waterfall and reservoir, hiding the water line.

◀ In nature water in a stream slices through the earth. Excavate deep enough for streams and waterfalls for the gushing water to be slightly below grade. Use stones of various sizes when edging a water feature.

DRY CREEK BEDS

A dry creek bed should look like a stream that has run dry. Remove all weeds from the area, by either spraying with weed killer or pulling by hand. Cover the entire creek bed area with landscape fabric for a weed barrier. Place a 1-inch layer of clean gravel or gravel and sand mix on top of the weed barrier so that the bottoms of the stones nestle in, and appear to be slightly indented in, the ground.

Place the stones as shown at *right*. A dry creek bed looks better if all or a portion of the bed conforms to a slope, even if just a slight one.

If the dry creek bed will help channel spring runoff or summer rains, install pond liner underlayment and rubber pond liner instead of the landscape fabric. Then carefully place the stones for the creek bed directly onto the liner. Fill in gaps between stones with smaller stones, finishing with pockets of clean gravel.

▶ If the bed will not carry moisture runoff, cover the area with landscape fabric, then add a 1-inch layer of pea gravel or gravel and sand mix. Airborne weed seeds will eventually germinate in a dry creek bed, so routine weeding will be necessary.

▼ Place large stones along the banks of the creek bed, but don't forget to mix in some larger stones throughout the middle as well. Don't keep an even width; streams tend to be wider around curves and narrower where they run relatively straight.

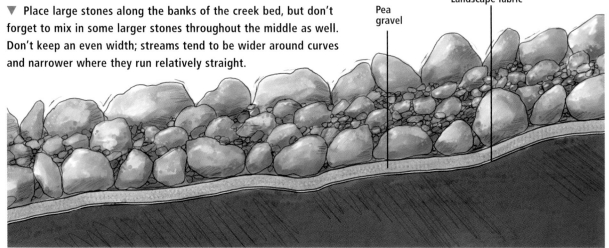

Pea gravel

Landscape fabric

CHAPTER HIGHLIGHTS

Complete your stone landscaping project with plants. This chapter reviews plants that will survive foot traffic on paths and patios and plants that grow nicely in crevices between rocks. There's also information about dwarf and spreading evergreens and water plants, plus some tips on planting and care.

COMPANION PLANTS

Stone and plants are perfect partners. Lush living plants change constantly, providing a counterpoint to the solid and enduring stone.

Wherever you live, there's an abundance of annuals, perennials, trees, and shrubs available to complement your new stone feature. When you add plantings to stone, work with plants appropriate for your area that you already know. There are no plants specifically prescribed for use with stone, so don't worry about making a mistake by planting something that doesn't belong in a stone landscape.

However there are plants that match the physical characteristics of stone landscape features. Plants that thrive under foot traffic in the gaps between flagstones, that climb stone walls, or that grow well in moist soils beside a pond or stream will help blend your new stone feature into older parts of the landscape.

This chapter shows some of the best and most readily available complementary plants for stone.

PLANTS THAT WITHSTAND FOOT TRAFFIC

Low-growing plants and groundcovers are great for gaps between stones in pathways and patios. Lawn grasses suitable for your area also work well. Snip or mow grasses or plants during the growing season to keep them from engulfing the path or patio.

BUGLEWEED

Ajuga reptans 'Chocolate Chip'

Moderate traffic, sun to part shade, Zones 4–9. Matting, quick spreader, 2 inches tall, with tiny, shiny, oval, brownish leaves. Has 3-inch spikes of blue flowers in spring. (Shown *below left*.)

SANDWORT

Arenaria montana

Moderate traffic, full sun, Zones 5–8. Mounding, fast-growing trailer, 2–4 inches tall, with narrow leaves. Bears small white flowers in early summer.

DWARF ORANGE WALLFLOWER

Erysimum kotschyanum

Light traffic, sun to part shade, Zones 4–10. Matting, moderate spreader, 1–3 inches tall, with jagged, light green leaves. Intense orange flowers blossom in early spring.

IRISH MOSS

Sagina subulata

Heavy traffic, sun to part shade, Zones 4–10. Mounding, mosslike foliage, ¼–½ inch tall. Tiny star-shaped flowers bloom white in spring. Avoid hot afternoon sun.

MINIATURE STONECROP

Sedum requienii

Heavy traffic, sun, Zones 4–8. Matting, slow-growing succulent, ½–1 inch tall, with tiny green leaves. Drought tolerant. (Shown at *right*.)

CREEPING THYME

Thymus doerfleri 'Bressingham Pink'

Moderate traffic, sun to light shade, Zones 4–9. Matting, moderate spreader, 2 inches tall, with light green, finely-textured leaves. Displays hot pink flowers in midsummer.

WOOLLY THYME

Thymus pseudolanuginosus

Moderate to heavy traffic, sun to part sun, Zones 6–9. Matting, moderate spreader, 3 inches tall, with dusty gray foliage. Has pink flowers in summer. Requires good drainage (Shown *below*.)

DWARF PERIWINKLE

Vinca minor

Heavy foot traffic, partial shade, Zones 5–9. Arching, moderate spreader, 5 inches tall, with dark, shiny, oval leaves. Its pinwheel-shaped flowers are lavender or white.

VELVET SEDGE

Carex speciosa 'Velebit Humilis'

Heavy traffic, sun to part shade, Zones 4–10. Mounding, ornamental sedge grass, 4–6 inches tall. Creamy flower heads appear in late spring.

PLANTS THAT GROW IN CREVICES

Plants that grow in the gaps between the stones of a dry-stacked retaining wall or freestanding wall soften the wall's appearance. Randomly placed plants accent and naturalize the stone face.

Plants shown on these pages can grow in small amounts of soil packed into crevices and cracks in stone walls and ruins. Keep the soil moist while plants are becoming established and during dry periods.

ROCKCRESS

Arabis spp.

Sun, medium to dry soil, Zones 4–7. Forms sprawling 6-inch rosettes of small, grayish green leaves. Bears fragrant, 1/2-inch, four-petaled white flowers in spring. An ideal plant for walls. (Shown *below*.)

SUN ROSE

Helianthemum nummularium

Sun, medium to dry soil, Zones 5–7. Low-growing, woody, shrublike plant with 8- to 12-inch lance-shaped evergreen foliage. Spread reaches 2–3 feet. Roselike 1-inch flowers bloom freely for up to two months, beginning in late spring. (Shown *above left*.)

CLIMBING PLANTS

Planted at the base of a stone feature, these plants will climb the stone face with either sticky tendrils or aerial roots. To train them, secure the plant to the wall with wires bent to form long staples.

■ CREEPING FIG

Ficus pumila

Part to full shade, Zones 9–10. Fast-growing vine with small, light green, oval leaves that stay flat against walls.

■ ENGLISH IVY

Hedera helix

Part to full shade, Zones 6–9. Fast growing vine with lobed, 3-inch, dark green leaves with white veins.

■ CLIMBING HYDRANGEA

Hydrangea anomala

Sun to light shade, Zones 4–9. Moderate-growing, woody vine with dark green leaves and small white flowers.

■ BOSTON IVY

Parthenocissus tricuspidata

Sun to light shade, Zones 3–9. Fast-growing, woody vine with large, maplelike leaves that turn bronze in the fall.

CREEPING PHLOX

Phlox stolonifera

Sun, medium moist soil, Zones 3–9. Forms a low, sprawling mat of narrow, linear green leaves, spreading to 2 feet wide. Tubular, deep pink flowers appear in spring. Ideal for walls. (Shown *above*.)

STONECROP

Sedum album 'Coral Carpet'

Sun, medium to dry soil, Zones 3–9. Quickly forms 3- to 6-inch mat of small, rounded, fleshy, coral-colored leaves that mature to bright green in summer, then turn reddish bronze in late fall. Bears clusters of tiny white or pale pink flowers in early summer. Ideal plant for walls.

WATER PLANTS

Water plants add an exotic touch to a pond. Any size of pond can become the focal point of a garden when it contains water plants. Local vendors can advise you on growing and winter care. Here are some reliable favorites:

GOLDEN VARIEGATED SWEET FLAG

Acorus gramineus variegatus 'Ogon'

Sun to part shade, Zones 6–11. Features narrow, upright ribbons of green foliage tinged with yellow stripes.

ARROWHEAD

Sagittaria latifolia

Sun, Zones 6–9. Tall stalk–up to 4 feet–rises from large, triangular basal leaves with white, 3/4-inch flowers in whorls of three. Flowers July–September.

LOTUS

Nelumbo nucifera

Sun, Zones 7–11. Can reach 12 inches across and grow up to 8 inches above the water surface. Initial large, rounded leaves lie flat on water followed by leaves that rise above. Blooms in midsummer. Delicate, upward-facing flower petals are pink, turning to white near the base, with a yellow center. (Shown *above.*)

DWARF UMBRELLA PALM

Cyperus alternifolius

Sun to shade, Zones 7–11. Arching, triangular stalks 18–30 inches tall support long, narrow leaves resembling the struts of an umbrella. Insignificant flowering. Invasive; do not allow into waterways.

WATER LILY

Nymphaea spp.

Sun, Zones 3–11 (species vary). A large, diverse family of water plants known for their flat, circular leaves and fragrant, multipetaled blooms. Tropical water lilies like the 'Mrs. Edwards Whitaker' cultivar, *opposite*, can spread 3–12 feet, and are grown as annuals in most climates. Hardy water lilies like the 'Hermine' cultivar, shown *above*, spread 3–12 feet and can overwinter in deep ponds in all but the northernmost regions.

WATER PARSLEY

Oenanthe spp.

Sun to part shade, Zones 5–11. Aromatic, lobed, finely cut foliage resembling parsley is attractive all season. Masses of tiny white flowers bloom in spring and fall. Some varieties have variegated leaves tipped with pink.

YELLOW FLAG

Iris pseudacorus

Sun to part shade, Zones 4–11. Yellow flowers appear in spring with 24–36-inch-tall green, swordlike foliage.

DWARF AND SPREADING EVERGREENS

Evergreens and stone seem to go together naturally. The color and foliage of evergreens add year-round interest to a stone feature. Dwarf evergreens can be a perfect backdrop for pathways, patios, ponds, and waterfalls. Low-growing, spreading evergreens look wonderful in rock gardens and trailing down retaining walls.

GLOBE BLUE SPRUCE

Picea pungens 'Glauca Globosa'

Sun, Zones 3–9. This bright blue, dwarf globe spruce matures to 4 feet high and wide. (Shown *above.*)

PINE

Pinus spp.

Sun, Zones 2–10 (depending on variety). *Pinus banksiana* 'Uncle Fogey' is a graceful, weeping small tree, maturing at 6 feet, that complements rock outcroppings, stone walls, and larger rock gardens. *P. mugo* (mugho pine) has a rounded, tufted appearance and can be kept small with regular shearing. (Shown *above.*)

ALPINE FIR

Abies lasiocarpa var. *arizonica* 'Compacta'

Sun, Zones 3–9. This conical tree can reach 8 feet tall and have a 4-foot spread. The tree is dense, with blue, sprucelike needles.

WHITE FIR

Abies concolor 'Compacta'

Sun, Zones 3–9. Short, blue-gray needles characterize this billowy tree that matures to 5 feet tall with a spread of 4 feet.

JUNIPER

Juniperus spp.

Sun, Zones 2–10 (depending on variety). Dozens of varieties to choose from. *Juniperus sabina* includes 'Calgary Carpet,' a low, tough, spreading (up to 4 feet) juniper with rich green needles. *J. procumbens* 'Nana' has gray-green needles and a mounded, layering growth pattern that is ideal for rock gardens.

J. horizontalis (creeping juniper) is a group of very hardy spreaders that includes 'Blue Prince' and 'Prince of Wales.' *J. scopulorum* features upright, conical varieties from 3–12 feet tall, with needles of a rich blue-silver color. (Creeping juniper shown at *right.*)

YEW

Taxus spp.

Sun to full shade, Zones 3–10. Available in a variety of forms, from upright conical to low spreading, all with short, dark green needles. Very reliable in shade. *Taxus cuspidata* 'Emerald Spreader' (Japanese yew) grows to just 3 feet tall but spreads to 10 feet; *T. cuspidata* 'Capitata' (Japanese upright yew) is pyramidal and can grow to 15 feet tall.

PLANTING YOUR GARDEN

Preparing your garden for planting is just as important as preparing your house for painting. Scraping, washing, and priming are more important (and often more time consuming) than the painting that follows. This same principle applies to planting a garden.

Good soil is the key to successful gardening. After a stone project is completed, the soil surrounding the project area often has been disrupted, compacted, graded, or in other ways altered. Subsoil, sand, or cement may have become mixed in with the topsoil. Putting plants into the ground without properly preparing the

soil can result in a sickly garden that detracts from, rather than accents, your stonework.

Good garden soil contains 80 to 90 percent black mineral soil and 10 to 20 percent organic matter. Coarse sand should be added to make up about 5 percent of the finished mix. Start your garden preparation by determining what kind of soil you have. Dig a hole 18 inches deep and look at the soil layers. Do you have a few inches of black topsoil, or a foot of it? See whether there's a sandy silt, a gravel mix, or dense clay beneath the topsoil.

Amend your soil so the proper mix of soil and organic matter is at least 16 inches deep.

▶ The first step in preparing a garden is to till the soil. Dig as deep as the machine will go.

Here's one way to do that:

■ Rototill the area to the tiller's maximum depth, then remove the loosened soil and add a 4-inch layer of organic matter, such as compost, peat moss, composted manure, or a mix of all three.

■ Till the area again. Replace about one half of the soil that was removed, and add a 2-inch layer of organic matter.

■ Till one more time. You will have excess soil because of the organic material you added. Either distribute this soil elsewhere, or raise the bed by edging it with stone. If you do that, place your edging, put all the soil back, and add more organic matter before the final tilling.

You can do two things for a heavy clay soil: remove it or amend it. You may save time and money by hiring a landscaper to remove all the clay where you want a garden. Then buy black dirt, organic matter, and sand to make a good

◀ Good garden loam is rich and crumbly. Organic matter in the soil helps drainage and retains moisture for plant roots.

gardening mix.

The other option is to rototill clay areas while adding plenty of organic material– 40 percent or more. Never add sand when amending clay soil; the result will be much like concrete.

TEST YOUR SOIL

A soil test will help determine what improvement your soil needs. Ask your state university's county extension office for a soil test kit. Submit your soil, and for a nominal fee you will receive a report showing your soil's organic content and overall composition. Nutrient deficiencies and steps you can take to correct them will also be noted. This type of test is more comprehensive than do-it-yourself tests.

DESIGN AND PLANTING TIPS

Consider the color, shape, and texture of the stone in your landscape when you select plants to grow on or near it. Contrasts of shapes, sizes, and colors add vitality to garden design.

A hosta with blue leaves planted next to edging of gray-blue traprock will almost disappear, for instance. But a hosta with yellow or gold variegation on the leaves will stand out against the same edging because of the color contrast between the stone and the leaves. The stone will show up better too. The jagged, intricate foliage of ferns looks much better in front of a wall constructed of round fieldstones than does a plant with large, rounded leaves.

Combine plants, including trees and shrubs, to create strong contrasts between the size, shape, and color of their leaves. Color of bloom, while important, is a secondary consideration. Experienced gardeners often wait until late in the season to purchase perennials, trees, and shrubs, because the plants they buy have grown taller and have greater foliage. Arrange plants in combinations while they are still in their pots, so

■ Leave gaps in stone features for planting. Add good soil between the stones, if necessary, and scoop out a place for the plant, as shown *below left*. Place a small stone in front of the plant to hold it and the soil in place, as shown *below*. Keep the plants watered but not soggy; there may not be much soil around their roots.

PLANTING TREES AND SHRUBS

▲ **Color, texture, height, and plant diversity are all elements of this attractive pond and garden.**

you can easily move them around to try different foliage and height combinations.

If you add soil to the cracks and crevices of walls or to the gaps between stones in patios and pathways, make sure it's good gardening soil that has been properly amended. Perennials and annuals grown in these areas haven't much room to develop roots, so good soil is essential.

Trees and shrubs need good soil like other garden plants. You can usually amend the soil for a tree or shrub just in the planting hole rather than tilling a large area around the tree. Here are some other tips for tree planting:

■ Dig the planting hole as wide as possible. The old rule about digging a hole twice as wide as the tree's container is now considered the bare minimum. It's better to dig a wider hole, or at least to loosen the soil surrounding the hole with a rototiller or shovel.

■ Dig the hole 1 to 3 inches less than the depth of the soil in the container. This raises the plant up just a little bit after planting. Planting high encourages roots to grow down and out instead of girdling the tree or shrub.

■ Place the plant in the hole, fill the hole halfway with the soil that was removed, and tamp it in lightly with your feet. Put 2 inches of water into the hole, wait for it to drain completely, then add the rest of the soil. Tamp this in lightly, then water again. Mulch with a 3-inch layer of shredded bark or wood chips across the area, keeping the mulch 2 inches away from the trunk of the tree or shrub.

■ During the first two years, water trees and shrubs thoroughly once a week when it doesn't rain. Water during the winter, too, when there's a sunny day with no snow cover.

◀ **Fill the planting hole for a tree halfway with soil, then add water. As the water drains away, it moistens and helps settle the soil.**

GLOSSARY

A-D

Aerate To supply air to the water in a pond or pool. Aeration helps prevent oxygen depletion and water stagnation.

Algae Plants or plantlike organisms that grow in ponds. Some algae are beneficial; others, such as floating phytoplankton and green string algae, are not. Abundant algae turn the water murky green; there's too much if you can't see your hand through 12 inches of water. Consult a pond supply dealer for algae control.

Annuals Plants that live for one growing season then die. Annuals are replanted each spring. Some annuals sow their own seeds to regenerate each season. (See *perennials.*)

Batter The inward slope from bottom to top on the face of a wall.

Batter gauge A tapered board attached to a level to measure the batter of a wall. (See *pages 102–103.*)

Bluestone A dark, blue-gray granite.

Bonding stone A long stone that spans from one face to the other to tie a wall together. Also called a *bondstone.*

Boulder A large stone, usually round or egg-shaped, weathered and worn smooth.

Bowl fountain A water feature with one or more bowls, usually on a central stem. Water, which sometimes sprays into the air from the top, spills from one bowl to the next, and often pours into a pool beneath the fountain.

Calcite marble A decorative stone of crystalline calcium carbonate that is embedded with colored silicates.

Capstone The top course of stone on a wall or the flat top stone on a pillar or post.

Cobblestone A medium-size, naturally rounded stone used for paving.

Cut stone Quarried stone cut to uniform-size squares and rectangles for paving.

Diopside A decorative green to white stone consisting of pyroxene.

Dry-laid A stone patio or path laid without mortar, usually on a sand and gravel base.

Dry-stacked A wall constructed of stacked stones without mortar.

F-K

Fieldstone Smooth granite rocks, round or oblong, 6 to 24 inches in diameter, found on the ground or partially buried.

Fines Powdery residue from mechanical crushing, found in crushed gravels.

Flagstone Flat slabs of limestone, quartz, sandstone, or other kinds of stone. The slabs are often large, but are easy to split. Flagstone is used for paths, patios, walls, and other projects.

Footing A below-grade concrete slab or compacted gravel surface that supports a stone wall or other structure.

Fossilized rock Decorative rock with fossilized remains of flora or fauna.

GFCI Ground fault circuit interrupter, a device that instantly cuts off electricity when it senses an unbalanced flow in the hot and neutral wires, as in a short circuit. The pump for a water feature must be plugged into a GFCI for safety.

Grade (noun) The level of the ground at a project site. (verb) To change, level, or smooth the surface of the ground.

Granite Hard, natural, igneous rock that contains quartz and forms of crystalline feldspar.

Gravel Small, loose rocks. *Natural gravel* often comes from rivers; rocks are smooth and rounded. The rocks in *crushed gravel*, made by mechanically crushing larger rocks, are more irregular and jagged.

Hisingerite A decorative rock; black to brownish black with yellowish brown streaking.

L–P

Landing An intermediate surface between stairs or staircases. Stairs often change direction at a landing.

Landscape fabric A nonwoven fabric that allows water and air to pass through but blocks weed growth. Better to use than plastic sheeting for landscape construction.

Limestone A versatile stone made mostly of calcium carbonate, formed mainly from shells and other organic remains.

Lip stone The stone water flows over for a waterfall. Also called *lip rock*.

Mortar A mixture of one part sand, one part portland cement, and enough water to make a thick paste; used to set stone for patios, walls, and other projects and as grout between stones.

Mosaic A surface of small stones of various colors and other materials, usually set in mortar.

Outcropping A boulder placed in a landscape so it looks like a natural occurrence.

Paver Stone cut to a uniform size for use in paths or patios.

Perennials Plants that live more than one season. Perennials don't need to be replanted every year. (See *annuals*.)

Pond liner Rubber sheeting placed in a pond excavation to prevent water from draining through the soil. The flexible liner conforms to surface contours, so you can make ledges for plant containers inside the pond.

Primary pathway A main travel route through the yard, such as from the driveway or public sidewalk to the front door of the house.

Q–W

Quarried Stone broken from a large, natural deposit, usually in an open excavation. Limestone, slate, and others are quarried.

Quartzite Hard, light-colored, natural rock made of quartz and sandstone particles. Usually looks crystalline and sparkly on broken faces.

Retaining wall A wall constructed to prevent soil behind it from sliding down a slope.

Riprap Rough, jagged pieces of quarried stone, which can be stacked to make rustic walls. Smaller than traprock, riprap is commonly used in civil engineering to stabilize slopes, streambanks, and similar projects. (See *traprock*.)

Rock garden A landscape feature that combines stone and plants.

Rubble Mixed rocks of various shapes and sizes used to fill between faces of a wall.

Ruin A new stone feature constructed to look like one that has crumbled with age.

Sandstone A sedimentary rock that usually contains quartz sand. Flagstones are often large pieces of sandstone.

Scree A feature that resembles the piles of loose stones found in nature at the foot of a hill or the bottom of a cliff.

Screed (noun) A straight board that is pulled over sand or concrete to level the surface. (verb) To level a surface with a screed.

Secondary pathway A path that is not a main travel route through a landscape, such as a path through a flower garden.

Slab A stone feature arranged to resemble a large, single stone outcropping that has split into fragments over time.

Slate Dense stone formed in nature by compression of sedimentary rock; flagstones are often large pieces of slate.

Statuary fountain A fountain that looks like a classical statue of a human figure. Water can pour from an urn held by the figure.

Stepper A piece of flagstone small enough to use as a stepping-stone. (See *stepping-stone.*)

Stepping-stone A flat stone large enough for a footstep, used to construct a path.

Stone step Stone cut or split to size for use as a step or in a staircase.

Terra-cotta Brownish orange fired clay used to make decorative plant containers and statuary.

Traprock Large quarried rocks with jagged shapes and rough surfaces, used for wall construction. Commonly used in highway construction. (See *riprap.*)

Tumbled stone Rocks that have been smoothed by rotating a quantity of them in a revolving cylinder.

Underlayment A nonwoven synthetic fabric placed under a rubber pond liner to prevent punctures and tears.

Wallstone Quarried rock, usually limestone, cut into rough blocks for wall construction.

METRIC CONVERSIONS

U.S. Units to Metric Equivalents			Metric Units to U.S. Equivalents		
To Convert From	Multiply By	To Get	To Convert From	Multiply By	To Get
Inches	25.4	Millimeters	Millimeters	0.0394	Inches
Inches	2.54	Centimeters	Centimeters	0.3937	Inches
Feet	30.48	Centimeters	Centimeters	0.0328	Feet
Feet	0.3048	Meters	Meters	3.2808	Feet
Yards	0.9144	Meters	Meters	1.0936	Yards
Square inches	6.4516	Square centimeters	Square centimeters	0.1550	Square inches
Square feet	0.0929	Square meters	Square meters	10.764	Square feet
Square yards	0.8361	Square meters	Square meters	1.1960	Square yards
Acres	0.4047	Hectares	Hectares	2.4711	Acres
Cubic inches	16.387	Cubic centimeters	Cubic centimeters	0.0610	Cubic inches
Cubic feet	0.0283	Cubic meters	Cubic meters	35.315	Cubic feet
Cubic feet	28.316	Liters	Liters	0.0353	Cubic feet
Cubic yards	0.7646	Cubic meters	Cubic meters	1.308	Cubic yards
Cubic yards	764.55	Liters	Liters	0.0013	Cubic yards

To convert from degrees Fahrenheit (F) to degrees Celsius (C), first subtract 32, then multiply by $\frac{5}{9}$.

To convert from degrees Celsius to degrees Fahrenheit, multiply by $\frac{9}{5}$, then add 32.

USDA PLANT HARDINESS ZONE MAP

This map of climate zones helps you select plants for your garden that will survive a typical winter in your region. The United States Department of Agriculture (USDA) developed the map, basing the zones on the lowest recorded temperatures across North America. Zone 1 is the coldest area and Zone 11 is the warmest.

Plants are classified by the coldest temperature and zone they can endure. For example, plants hardy to Zone 6 survive where winter temperatures drop to –10° F. Those hardy to Zone 8 die long before it's that cold. These plants may grow in colder regions but must be replaced each year. Plants rated for a range of hardiness zones can usually survive winter in the coldest region as well as tolerate the summer heat of the warmest one.

To find your hardiness zone, note the approximate location of your community on the map, then match the color band marking that area to the key.

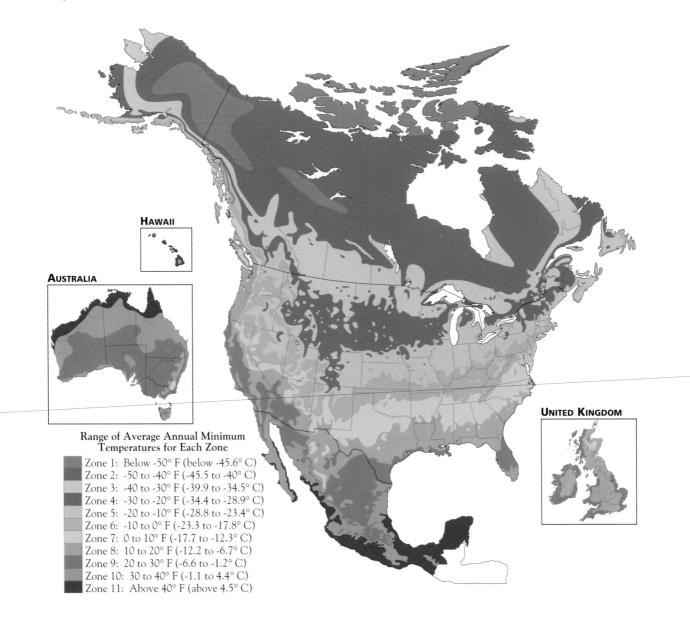

HAWAII

AUSTRALIA

UNITED KINGDOM

Range of Average Annual Minimum Temperatures for Each Zone

Zone 1: Below -50° F (below -45.6° C)
Zone 2: -50 to -40° F (-45.5 to -40° C)
Zone 3: -40 to -30° F (-39.9 to -34.5° C)
Zone 4: -30 to -20° F (-34.4 to -28.9° C)
Zone 5: -20 to -10° F (-28.8 to -23.4° C)
Zone 6: -10 to 0° F (-23.3 to -17.8° C)
Zone 7: 0 to 10° F (-17.7 to -12.3° C)
Zone 8: 10 to 20° F (-12.2 to -6.7° C)
Zone 9: 20 to 30° F (-6.6 to -1.2° C)
Zone 10: 30 to 40° F (-1.1 to 4.4° C)
Zone 11: Above 40° F (above 4.5° C)

INDEX